That's No Problem!
A Problem-Free Approach to Problem Solving

Dr. Marlene Caroselli

American Media Publishing
4900 University Avenue
West Des Moines, Iowa 50266-6769 U.S.A.
800/262-2557

That's No Problem!
A Problem-Free Approach to Problem Solving

Dr. Marlene Caroselli
Copyright © 1997 by American Media Incorporated

All rights reserved. No part of this publication may be reproduced, stored in a retrieval system, or transmitted, in any form or by any means, electronic, mechanical, photocopying, recording, or otherwise, without the prior written permission of the publisher.

This publication is designed to provide accurate and authoritative information in regard to the subject matter covered. It is sold with the understanding that neither the author nor the publisher is engaged in rendering legal, accounting, or other professional service. If legal advice or other expert assistance is required, the services of a competent professional person should be sought.

Credits:
American Media Publishing:	Art Bauer
	Todd McDonald
Managing Editor:	Karen Massetti Miller
Editor:	Jill J. Jensen
Designer:	Gayle O'Brien
Cover Design:	Polly Beaver

Published by American Media Inc.
4900 University Avenue
West Des Moines, IA 50266-6769

Library of Congress Card Number 97-70155
Caroselli, Marlene
That's No Problem! A Problem-Free Approach to Problem Solving

Printed in the United States of America
ISBN 1-884926-74-6

Introduction

Herman Melville noted that "a smooth sea never made a successful sailor." If our lives were free of problems, they would not only be boring, but they would also deny us the chance to develop our talents. Through solving problems, we discover new approaches, uncover new opportunities, and recover lost confidence. But for many people, the process of solving problems is a haphazard one.

By following the sequential steps in this book, you will no longer solve problems haphazardly. If you adopt these recommendations and ideas, you will emerge with a definite plan for tackling the decisions you need to make, the problems you need to solve, and the goals you want to reach. Once you know the steps, all you have to do is follow them.

Begin with the Self-Assessment. It provides insights into the methods you currently employ and the areas that need further development. Continue with the exercises in each chapter, and by the end of the book, you will have found an approach that works for you.

Equipped with an internal mechanism for dissecting problems and solving them, you will be able to share J. C. Penney's attitude toward difficulties: "I am grateful for all my problems. After each one was overcome, I became stronger and more able to meet those that were still to come. I grew in all my difficulties."

About the Author

Dr. Marlene Caroselli founded the Center for Professional Development in 1984 to help working adults improve their communication, managerial, and leadership skills. She has conducted training seminars for a number of major corporations and the federal government and has also served as an adjunct faculty member at UCLA and National University. Besides lecturing in more than half the states in the United States, Dr. Caroselli has also conducted workshops in Guam, Canada, Singapore, and Brazil.

Dr. Caroselli has published several books on business-related issues. Her articles frequently appear in *National Business Employee Weekly, International Customer Service Association Journal,* and Stephen Covey's *Executive Excellence.* Dr. Caroselli also delivers keynote addresses on a number of topics.

Self-Assessment

This assessment follows the sequential steps of problem solving. It will further your knowledge about your problem-solving style in general and the improvements that may be needed in particular stages. Note that by *problem,* we do not mean minor problems, such as a schedule conflict. Rather, the problems we will take through the process in this book are work-related problems of some significance.

Circle the number that best characterizes your normal practice. If the item reflects something you never do, circle *1;* if you sometimes do it, circle *2;* and so on. Total your scores for the individual sections of the assessment, then add them together to determine your overall total at the end of the assessment.

	Never	Sometimes	Often	Always
Problem Definition Total:_____				
1. I begin the problem-solving process by defining the problem.	1	2	3	4
2. I ask others to restate the problem as they see it.	1	2	3	4
3. I put the problem in writing.	1	2	3	4
4. It takes a while to define the problem I have to solve.	1	2	3	4
Generation of Solutions Total:_____				
1. I consider how the problem has been solved in the past.	1	2	3	4
2. Ideas for possible solutions come to me quickly.	1	2	3	4
3. I write down the possible answers.	1	2	3	4
4. I look outside my field for possible answers.	1	2	3	4
Review of Available Tools Total:_____				
1. As a team, we use consensus tools for list reduction.	1	2	3	4
2. I use tools like the Fishbone to stratify possibilities.	1	2	3	4
3. I validate my own "hunches" about possible solutions.	1	2	3	4

	Never	Sometimes	Often	Always

4. I use tools or forms for gathering data.   1   2   3   4

Selection of a Possible Solution   Total:_____
1. I involve others in solving work-related problems.   1   2   3   4

2. I keep the mission in mind when choosing a solution.   1   2   3   4

3. I use criteria for selection of a possible solution.   1   2   3   4

4. I consider consequences in my selection.   1   2   3   4

Implementation of the Solution   Total:_____
1. I determine what resources are available for implementation.   1   2   3   4

2. I determine in advance who will be impacted by the solution.   1   2   3   4

3. I meet with those who will be impacted.   1   2   3   4

4. I have a written plan/schedule for implementation.   1   2   3   4

Evaluation of the Solution   Total:_____
1. I track the pre- and postsolution results.   1   2   3   4

2. I assemble those whose input can help develop "the big picture."   1   2   3   4

3. I attempt to salvage before abandoning the solution.   1   2   3   4

4. I keep a log of "lessons learned."   1   2   3   4

Overall Total:_____

I track the outcomes of intuitively made decisions.   Yes or No? _____

Interpretation

Add your circled numbers. What is your overall total? _____ If you answered the very last question *Yes,* add another four points. What is the total now? _____

If your score was above 80, you are already quite adept at problem solving. But no one is perfect. There is still much more to learn about the process.

If you scored between 60 and 79, you could be considered average in terms of your problem-solving efficiency. Those people who buy books and attend classes related to self-improvement, though, are seldom average in their desire to learn. Continue to read and develop your skills in the subsequent chapters.

A score below 59 indicates you are relatively new to the problem-solving process and consequently have much to learn about the mastery of it. Absorb as much as you can and then check with others periodically to see if they have noticed improvement.

Review your individual scores for each of the six categories of the assessment. Which category had the highest score? _____
Which had the lowest? _____

Your highest category is clearly one in which you are already proficient; you are already performing the steps associated with that stage of the problem-solving process. Your lowest category score, however, is the one to which you should give special attention as you continue with the following chapters.

Table of Contents

Chapter One
Determining Your Problem-Solving Style   10

Two Approaches to Problem Solving	10
Which Approach Do You Prefer?	13
Which Approach Works Best When?	15
Developing Your Less-Favored Style	17
Chapter Summary	19
Self-Check: Chapter 1 Review	20

Chapter Two
Step 1: Defining the Problem   22

Taking a Positive Perspective	23
Determining the Amount of Time to Spend on a Problem	25
Defining the Problem	25
Identifying the Problem and Its Causes	26
Considering a Problem from Multiple Perspectives	30
Creating a Working Definition of the Problem	33
Chapter Summary	34
Self-Check: Chapter 2 Review	36

Chapter Three
Step 2: Generating Solutions   38

Unleashing Your Creativity	38
Brainstorming for Solutions	39
Using the Janusian Technique to See Opposite Sides of a Problem	41
Synthesizing Ideas from Diverse Disciplines to Gain New Insights	44
Creating Metaphors to Place Problems in New Contexts	46
Using the Full-Circle Method to Generate New Ideas	48
Chapter Summary	50
Self-Check: Chapter 3 Review	51

Chapter Four
Working with Teams   52

Characteristics of Successful Teams	53
Techniques Used by High-Performance Teams	58
Combining Task and Maintenance Behaviors	59
Consensus Tools Used by Teams	62
Chapter Summary	65
Self-Check: Chapter 4 Review	67

Table of Contents

Chapter Five
Step 3: Selecting a Solution   68
    Grouping Alternatives with the Affinity Diagram   69
    Evaluating Major Issues with the Comparative Valuation Process   72
    Thinking "Outside the Box"   82
    Considering the Consequences of Your Actions   84
    Chapter Summary   86
    Self-Check: Chapter 5 Review   88

Chapter Six
Step 4: Implementing the Solution   90
    Overcoming Resistance with Lewin's Change Model   91
    Implementing Solutions with the 5-X Strategy   94
    Chapter Summary   98
    Self-Check: Chapter 6 Review   99

Chapter Seven
Step 5: Evaluating the Solution   100
    Tracking Results   100
    Taking a Quantitative Approach: The Correlation Chart   101
    Taking a Qualitative Approach: The Focus Group   102
    Fine-Tuning Your Solution   105
    Compiling the Lessons You've Learned   106
    Following the Steps of the P-D-C-A Cycle   107
    Chapter Summary   108
    Self-Check: Chapter 7 Review   110

Chapter Eight
Step 6: Improving Continuously   112
    Continuous Improvement Through Benchmarking   113
    Setting "Stretch" Goals   115
    Chapter Summary   118
    Self-Check: Chapter 8 Review   119

Answers to Selected Exercises   120

● **Determining Your Problem-Solving Style**

Chapter *One*

Determining Your Problem-Solving Style

> ### Chapter Objectives
> ▶ Define *convergent* and *divergent* approaches to problem solving.
>
> ▶ Define *lateralized thinking*.
>
> ▶ Assess your own strengths and weakness regarding the two approaches.
>
> ▶ Solve problems by selecting the most appropriate approach.
>
> ▶ Use your less-favored style more often than you currently do.

Though we might sometimes think we'd like our lives to be problem-free, being alive means having problems. In fact, some people define life as a series of problems to be solved. The challenges these problems present give us the opportunity to learn and grow. Without them, our lives would be static.

Two Approaches to Problem Solving

Each day, we face hundreds of problems to solve and decisions to make. We can solve these problems systematically or creatively. Both approaches are necessary. Both are valued. But in a given situation, we may choose to emphasize one approach over the other.

Determining Your Problem-Solving Style

We can solve problems systematically by using the *convergent approach.* This is an analytical process that follows a series of steps to reach a solution.

1. Define the problem.
2. Generate solutions.
3. Select a solution.
4. Implement the solution.
5. Evaluate the solution.

The convergent approach is a logical, deliberate means of solving problems. This approach enables you to proceed along a defined path until the solution is achieved. It is used most frequently in scientific investigation.

In contrast, we can solve problems in a less structured, more creative way by using the *divergent approach.* The divergent approach calls on intuition and innovation, analogy and visualization, humor, and even absurdity. The divergent approach encourages spontaneity while the convergent approach moves quietly and determinedly toward a solution. In short, creativity diverges from the straight-and-narrow path that convergent thinking requires you to follow.

This book emphasizes the convergent approach to problem solving, and the book chapters are organized to reflect the steps in the convergent problem-solving process. However, we will also discuss creative techniques that can be used in less structured problem-solving situations.

> **The *convergent approach* to problem solving follows a series of steps to reach a solution.**

> **The *divergent approach* is a less structured, more creative means of problem solving.**

● Determining Your Problem-Solving Style

Take a Moment

This exercise illustrates how a problem can be solved by both convergent and divergent approaches. One approach, however, is clearly preferable because it is quicker. Imagine there are 8 executives in a conference room. Each executive shakes hands just once with each of the other executives. What is the total number of handshakes? _____

How Did You Solve the Problem?

If you are mathematically inclined and familiar with the term *factorial,* you probably used a simple formula and obtained the correct answer very quickly. The formula requires you to multiply the number of people (8) by the number of people minus one (7), and then divide the product by two in order to obtain the answer, in this case, 28. $\frac{n(n-1)}{2}$

The problem could also be solved in a more creative, visual manner, although this approach takes longer. The 8 people could be represented by circles and letters:

(Mr. A) → (Ms. B) → (Mr. C) → (Ms. D) →
(Mr. E) → (Ms. F) → (Mr. G) → (Ms. H)

As the arrows indicate, if Mr. A begins and shakes hands with each of the other executives, the total number of handshakes created by his efforts will be 7. Now Ms. B begins, but don't forget that she has already shaken with Mr. A, so she need only shake hands with C, D, E, F, G, and H—a total of 6 handshakes. The number will decrease by 1 as each person shakes, yielding a total of 28.

Determining Your Problem-Solving Style

Which Approach Do You Prefer?

If you solved the problem correctly, which method did you use: one that was more analytical or one that was more creative? Your choice reflects your preferred problem-solving style. Neither style is good nor bad, right nor wrong, efficient nor inefficient—you need to develop both. That is the purpose of this chapter and of this book: to increase your range of skills when it comes to solving problems.

Not all problems can be solved logically, nor can all be solved creatively. Using both sets of skills enables you to be more precise and more productive as you tackle thorny issues that confront you each day. You probably are already quite skilled in either the convergent or the divergent area. Ideally, you will develop your skills in both areas so you become *lateralized*, able to solve problems in both domains equally well. Lateralized thinkers can call upon either sphere, the logical or the imaginative, in order to find the answers they need.

If you didn't solve the problem correctly, at the very least, you have been exposed to two techniques for solving similar problems when you encounter them in the future.

Consider a second example. The answer to the following question is not as important as the way the answer came into your head. Remember how you determine the answer to this question:

- Recalling your early school years (say, from first grade to sixth grade), who was your favorite teacher?

Now, how did the answer come into your head? Did you see the teacher's face first? Did you remember his or her name first? Or did both the face and the name come to you simultaneously?

If you recalled the name, your thinking style most likely is convergent. If you visualized the face immediately, your preference is probably divergent. And, if both the name and face came to you together, you may have achieved the ideal state of being lateralized in your thinking.

> Ideally, you will develop your skills in both areas so you become *lateralized*, able to solve problems in both domains equally well.

Determining Your Problem-Solving Style

Take a Moment

Circle your answers to the following questions to obtain a fuller identification of your basic approach to solving problems. (There are no right or wrong answers.)

1. Sit in a relaxed position as you are reading this. Fold your hands in your lap. Now look at your hands. Which thumb is on top? (Was neither on top—you found the two thumbs beside each other?)   **left   right**

2. Assuming you could only have a foot patrol or a helicopter to locate a lost child in a park, which would you prefer?   **patrol   'copter**

3. When learning a new dance, is it easier for you to read about the steps or to watch as others perform the dance?   **read   watch**

4. Are you an organized person?   **yes   no**

5. Do you pride yourself on being prompt?   **yes   no**

6. When you purchase a new appliance, do you prefer to try to make it work on your own or are you inclined to read the instruction manual?   **try   read**

7. Do you prefer the status quo or do you welcome change?   **status quo   change**

8. When you are driving and pull over to ask directions, do you write down what the person tells you or simply try to "see" the route in your head?   **write   see**

Continued on next page

Determining Your Problem-Solving Style

> **Take a Moment** *(continued)*
>
> 9. In a class, do you take copious notes or listen and digest the information?   **notes   listen**
>
> 10. I like to collect "stuff."   **true   false**
>
> How many answers did you circle in the left column? _____
>
> How many answers did you circle in the right column? _____
>
> If you had an even (5–5) or nearly-even split (4–6 or 6–4), congratulations! It suggests you are lateralized in your approach to problems. (And if your thumbs in Question 1 were side by side, you are quite likely to be tapping into both kinds of problem-solving talents.) If the majority of your answers (7 or more) were in Column 1, you probably think in a linear fashion and prefer solving problems in a logical, analytical manner. With 7 or more answers in Column 2, you tend to be more creative and probably enjoy problems that require the generation of multiple ideas.

If you are lateralized, continue to develop your abilities in both areas: convergent and divergent. If you are convergent, gain practice with the recommendations for divergent thinking. And, if you favor divergent thinking, it's time for cerebral workouts that call on your reasoning talents.

Which Approach Works Best When?

How can you know which problem-solving technique to apply? Quite simply, when a single, predictable answer is needed, an answer that is clearly correct, use the convergent approach. Such an answer would be "42" in response to the question, "How much is 6 times 7?" No other (correct) answer is possible.

When facing problems where multiple solutions are possible, problems with no established formulas or precedents, take a divergent approach. An example of this type of problem would be creating a name for a restaurant you plan to open. Many situations emphasize one approach but require insights

When a single, predictable answer is needed, use the convergent approach. When facing problems where multiple solutions are possible, take a divergent approach.

Determining Your Problem-Solving Style

from a second. You might follow the steps of the convergent approach to solve a scientific problem, for example, but you also need the insights gained from a divergent approach to help generate new and interesting research questions and unique interpretations of data. This is why it is so important to develop your skills in both types of approaches.

Take a Moment

For the following problems, indicate which of the two approaches you would use to solve the problem. Use the letter C for Convergent and D for Divergent. If you can think of solutions that are both convergent and divergent, use the letter L to represent Lateralized answers. Answers appear on page 120.

1. Your boss has asked you to survey department members regarding the possibility of a lunchtime lecture series. She has also asked for a report on this.   **C   D   L**

2. You are thinking of buying a sports car rather than a van. You've decided to list the advantages and disadvantages of each.   **C   D   L**

3. You enjoy solving puzzles and recently came across this, which asks, "What is the next letter in this sequence: O T T F F S S E____?"   **C   D   L**

4. Your boss has asked you for ideas regarding possible topics for upcoming articles in the company newsletter.   **C   D   L**

5. You are a supervisor and have encountered a problem with a "difficult" employee. Now you are formulating a plan of action regarding this problem.   **C   D   L**

Determining Your Problem-Solving Style

Developing Your Less-Favored Style

By now you should have a good sense of the problem-solving approach you use most often. Keep on using it! But as you analyze problems, you will find that neither style should be used all the time. Ideally, you will become sufficiently lateralized to choose the approach (convergent or divergent) that best fits the problem to be solved.

Here is a list of exercises to help you achieve lateralization.

If you need to develop your convergent, or analytical skills:

- **Develop your ability to gauge time requirements.** Before beginning a project, estimate how long it will take for completion. Then, work to complete the project within that time frame. You can also estimate how long it will take to reach the next freeway exit, or how many minutes it will be before the next commercial comes on.

- **Learn more about finance.** If you work in an organization, ask questions about budgets and annual reports and profit-and-loss statements. If you work in your own company or if you are not working, take a course, read a book, or meet with a financial planner to acquire more information about microeconomics. As you gain understanding of financial concepts, your logical, linear thinking develops. Such thinking lies at the heart of convergent mental processing.

- **For two weeks, keep a log of the problems you solve each day and the method (if any) you use to solve them.** Include a column to show the results of each solution or decision. For problems you solve haphazardly, begin to use the specific problem-solving techniques presented in later chapters of this book.

- Read a biography of an outstanding scientist to develop an appreciation for analysis.

- **Clean off your desk and organize your files.** Having immediate access to the information you need increases the likelihood of your seeing the task through to completion. One of the problems experienced by many creative people is an unwillingness to follow through.

● Determining Your Problem-Solving Style

If you need to develop your divergent, or imaginative skills:

- **Engage in "What if . . ." thinking.** Speculate about possibilities that could occur in both your personal and professional life.

- **Take an art class or a music class.** Management guru Peter Drucker advises managers seeking excellence to learn how to play the violin.

- **Whenever you can, imagine the possibilities surrounding a given object.** How many different uses, for example, can you find for a lettuce leaf?

- **Combine two unlikely possibilities and seek a solution in their union.** Believe it or not, French botanist Henri Fabre's work with processionary caterpillars has profound implications for leaders. He found processionary caterpillars followed their leader to their death, despite the fact that food was inches away. Atypical realms will yield atypical but workable ideas.

- **Associate with creative people.** Watch them, listen to them, learn their habits, observe them at work, and ask about their talents. Experiment with applying your new insights to your own behavior.

As you develop your skills through these and other activities, you will find that both types of problem solving become easier and easier.

Determining Your Problem-Solving Style

Chapter Summary

Although we may wish our lives were problem-free, we face many different problems and decisions every day. The two main approaches we can use to solve problems are the convergent approach and the divergent approach.

- The *convergent approach* is a systematic, logical approach to problem solving that follows a series of steps.

  - Step 1: Define the problem.
  - Step 2: Generate solutions.
  - Step 3: Select a solution.
  - Step 4: Implement the solution.
  - Step 5: Evaluate the solution.

- The *divergent approach* is a creative approach to problem solving. It uses brainstorming, intuition, and spontaneity to generate unique, innovative solutions.

The convergent approach is most appropriate in situations where there is only one correct answer. The divergent approach is most appropriate in situations where no preexisting procedures or formulas exist. Many situations may require you to emphasize one approach while also adapting aspects of the other.

To be ready for any complicated situation, you need to develop skills in both types of problem solving. There are many exercises to help you develop your analytical and your creative skills.

The next chapters follow the steps of the convergent approach to problem solving. They also contain creative approaches that can be used in less-structured problem-solving situations. We'll begin with the first step of problem solving: defining the problem to be solved.

● **Determining Your Problem-Solving Style**

Self-Check: Chapter 1 Review

Answer the questions below. Suggested answers appear on page 120.

1. Define the following terms:

   a. *Convergent* _____

   b. *Divergent* _____

   c. *Lateralized* _____

2. What are the five steps in the convergent, or scientific method of solving problems?

   a. _____

   b. _____

   c. _____

   d. _____

   e. _____

3. Explain why being lateralized is better than exclusively using a convergent or divergent approach.

   _____

   _____

   _____

4. Name two things that will enhance your convergent skills.

   _____

   _____

Determining Your Problem-Solving Style

5. Name two things that will develop your ability to think divergently.

   _____

   _____

• **Step 1: Defining the Problem**

Chapter Two

Step 1: Defining the Problem

> **Chapter Objectives**
> ▶ Bring a positive perspective to a problem situation.
> ▶ Determine how much time to devote to solving a problem.
> ▶ Identify and describe individual problems that create complex problem situations.
> ▶ Use the Fishbone Diagram and the Five-Why Technique to identify problems.
> ▶ Understand the importance of considering a problem from multiple perspectives.

H. L. Mencken observed, "For every complex problem, there is one solution that is simple, neat—and wrong." The purpose of this book is to encourage you to slow down, give complex problems the attention they deserve, and be more analytical than intuitive in your efforts to find workable solutions.

As mentioned in the previous chapter, this book follows the steps of the convergent problem-solving process:

1. Define the problem.
2. Generate solutions.
3. Select a solution.
4. Implement the solution.
5. Evaluate the solution.

Step 1: Defining the Problem

As we move through the problem-solving process, we will consider an additional step: *improve continuously.* With this additional step, the problem-solving process becomes a cycle as we continually strive to identify new challenges and develop creative solutions that will help us improve performance and relationships. The cyclical nature of the problem-solving process is illustrated in the following diagram.

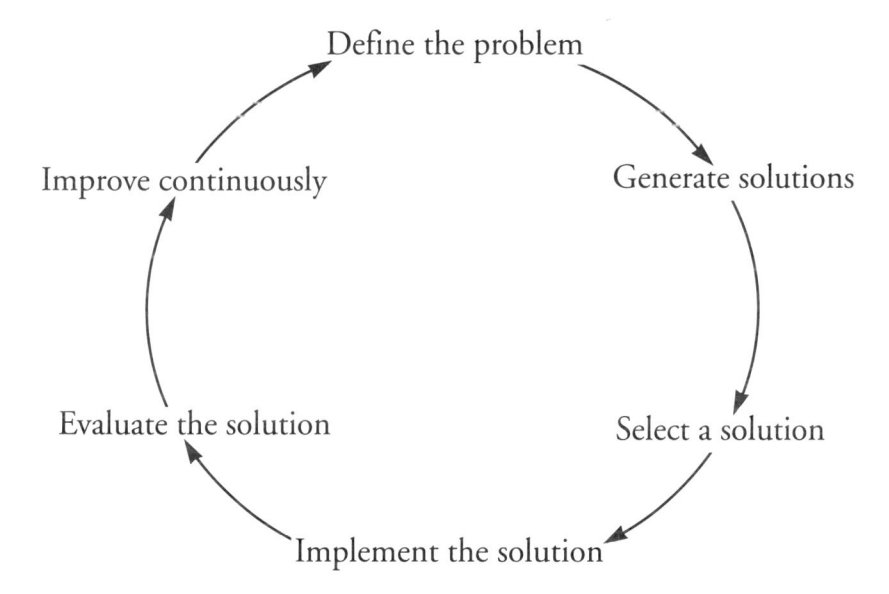

```
            Define the problem
                    ↑
Improve continuously      Generate solutions
                    
Evaluate the solution     Select a solution
                    ↑
            Implement the solution
```

As the diagram illustrates, defining the problem to be solved is an important early step in the problem-solving cycle. But before you begin, you need to establish a positive attitude toward problem solving.

Taking a Positive Perspective

■ "Oh, no! Not another fire to put out!"

How many times have you heard, or said, these words? Problem situations can often seem unpleasant or threatening, especially if an existing problem has created a negative atmosphere. The situation may be so bad that it's difficult to see a positive alternative.

It's easy to give in to this type of pessimism and fear, but doing so can cloud your thinking and keep you from generating an effective solution. Fight off negative thinking by taking a positive approach to problem solving.

Fight off negative thinking by taking a positive approach to problem solving.

Step 1: Defining the Problem

As you approach a new problem-solving situation, try using words like *challenge* and *opportunity* in relation to the word *problem*. In fact, these positive terms represent two questions that you should ask every time you sit down to solve a problem:

- How can this problem challenge us to greater achievement?

- What opportunities are embedded in this problem?

Take a Moment

Think of a significant work-related (or personal) problem you now face and briefly describe it.

_____

_____

Now, apply the answers from these positive-perspective questions to the problem you described:

- How could this problem challenge you to greater achievement?

   _____

   _____

- What opportunities lie embedded in this problem?

   _____

   _____

As you continue to develop your problem-solving skills, you may discover that you actually enjoy the opportunity to develop creative solutions to complex challenges!

Step 1: Defining the Problem

Determining the Amount of Time to Spend on a Problem

An important issue to consider as you begin the problem-solving process is how much time to spend solving a given problem. The answer to this question varies with the problem at hand.

Remember that efficient problem solvers don't spend "100 dollars worth of energy on a 10-cent problem." Try to determine how important the problem is to you or your organization, and organize your time accordingly. The question of where to go for the company holiday party would probably rate much lower than the problem of redesigning a production process to avoid costly errors.

> Try to determine how important the problem is to you or your organization, and organize your time accordingly.

You also need to decide how much of your available time to spend on various steps in the problem-solving process. Although you may think that generating solutions to the problem should take up the greatest amount of your time, the task of identifying and accurately defining the problem should consume about one-half the time allocated to the problem as a whole. So, for example, if your team meets for two hours to resolve a problem, approximately the first hour should be spent delineating what the actual problem is. With that in mind, let's consider how to identify and describe the problem to be solved.

Defining the Problem

"A problem well stated," American inventor Charles F. Kettering affirmed, "is a problem half solved." Whether you are working individually or as a team, clearly defining and stating your problem helps you develop the most effective solution possible.

Defining a problem may seem simple, but the process is actually quite involved, and it can be broken into the following steps:

1. Identify the problem and its causes.
2. Consider the problem from other perspectives.
3. Create a working definition of the problem.

Each step can be completed by problem solvers working alone or in a group.

Step 1: Defining the Problem

Identifying the Problem and Its Causes

Identifying our problem should be easy. After all, we all know what our problems are—or do we? Consider the following case study:

> **Case Study**
>
> ■ "I just don't know what I'm going to do," Jesse confided to her coworker Ron. "I'm not sure I can get through the next week."
>
> "What's the problem?" Ron asked.
>
> "It's all this stress I'm under," Jesse explained. "I just don't know if I can take it any more."
>
> "Stress is no fun," Ron replied, "but what's your problem?"
>
> "I just told you," Jesse said impatiently, "I'm under a lot of stress."
>
> "Stress is the symptom of a problem," Ron said, "and you won't be able to do anything about it until you identify the problems that are causing the stress."

General statements actually describe complex situations caused by multiple problems.

To Jesse, the statement "I'm under a lot of stress," seemed like the description of a problem. But general statements like that actually describe complex situations caused by multiple problems. To develop a more accurate picture of her situation, Jesse needs to ask questions that can help identify the smaller problems causing her stress. These questions include:

♦ What are possible causes of this situation?

♦ Which of these causes are problems in themselves?

♦ What concerns surround these problems?

♦ What aspects of this situation are not actual problems?

Questions like these help break a complicated situation into its component parts. Using a graphic to visualize a problem can also be helpful. One type of graphic that can help identify the parts of a complex situation is the *Fishbone Diagram*.

The Fishbone Diagram resembles a fish skeleton: the short arrows leading to the causes are ribs, and the long arrow leading to the final result is the spine. In the previous example, Jesse

Step 1: Defining the Problem

could use the Fishbone to help her visualize various types of problems that are causing her stress. Categories might include *work problems, health problems, money problems, aging parents, teenage children,* and *move to new community.* Visually, the breakdown looks like this:

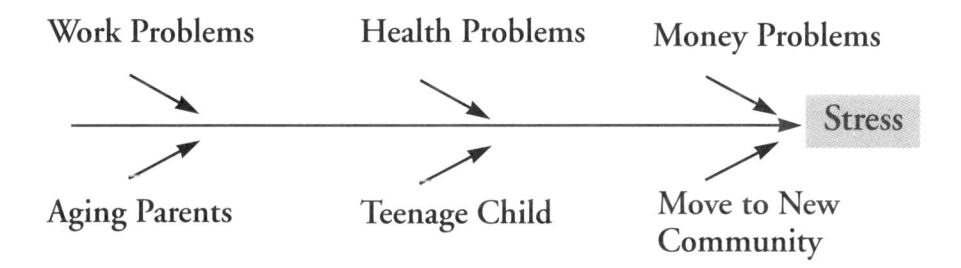

Work Problems   Health Problems   Money Problems

→ Stress

Aging Parents   Teenage Child   Move to New Community

Once you identify factors that cause the larger situation, you can begin to describe actual problems that need to be solved. For example, Jesse identified specific problems for each of her major categories.

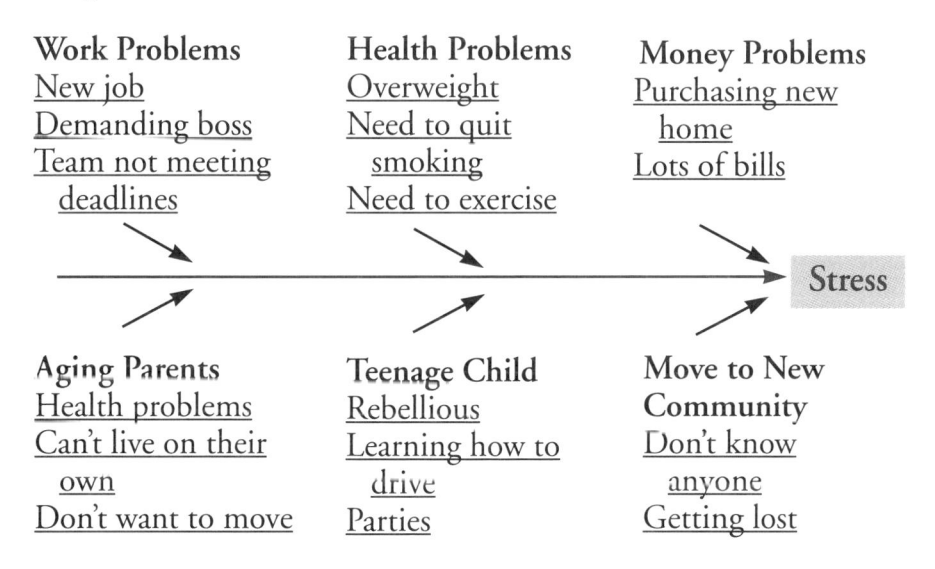

Work Problems
New job
Demanding boss
Team not meeting
   deadlines

Health Problems
Overweight
Need to quit
   smoking
Need to exercise

Money Problems
Purchasing new
   home
Lots of bills

→ Stress

Aging Parents
Health problems
Can't live on their
   own
Don't want to move

Teenage Child
Rebellious
Learning how to
   drive
Parties

Move to New Community
Don't know
   anyone
Getting lost

Setting her problems out in this way also gave Jesse the chance to prioritize them according to which were causing her the most stress. She decided that some of her problems, such as her move to a new community, would take care of themselves with time. Others, such as her family and work problems, needed to be solved quickly. Jesse developed these initial statements of her most important problems:

● Step 1: Defining the Problem

- ◆ My work team isn't completing its assignments quickly enough.
- ◆ My son refuses to obey rules.
- ◆ My parents are too ill to live on their own.

Identifying problems is just the beginning. Problem solvers should also look for root causes behind problems.

By breaking down her stress situation, Jesse developed a clearer understanding of the problems causing her stress. But identifying problems is just the beginning. Problem solvers should also look for root causes behind problems. Identifying root causes of problems helps you state your problem clearly and focus your problem-solving efforts where they will be most effective. One way you can identify the cause of a problem is by using the *Five-Why Technique*.

Take a Moment

Return to the problem you described in the exercise on page 24 and use the Fishbone Diagram below to break it down into smaller parts.

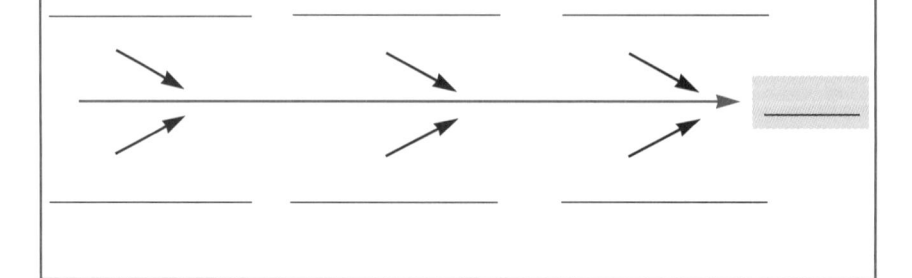

Using the Five-Why Technique to Identify Root Causes

A popular tool in Total Quality Management, the Five-Why Technique asks a series of *why* questions to identify individual problems and root causes. Often, it takes five *why* questions to identify the cause of a problem, although that number may vary. Let's return to our case study to see how Jesse could use the Five-Why Technique to get to the root cause of her problems at work.

Step 1: Defining the Problem

- Jesse just started a new job as a supervisor in the claims department of a health insurance company. Her team is responsible for processing claims that policyholders send requesting reimbursement for prescription medications. Lately, policyholders have complained that they must wait several months for reimbursement. Jesse decided to ask her team members why processing is so slow.

Case Study

Jesse:
We have a problem here. For the past year, we've received complaints that claims are taking several months to process. *Why* is this happening?

Employee 1:
We all work as hard as we can, and some of us put in overtime. It just takes a long time to get the claim information entered into the computer.

Jesse:
Why is it taking so long?

Employee 2:
The company has grown. There are a lot more forms than there used to be, and they're difficult to work with.

Jesse:
Why are they difficult?

Employee 3:
Sometimes customers don't fill them out correctly, and even when they do, it takes a long time for us to enter them on the computer.

Jesse:
Why do you think customers have problems with the forms?

Employee 2:
The instructions aren't very clear, and the print is small.

Jesse:
Is that *why* you're having trouble getting the information into the computer?

Employee 1:
Partly, plus we have different computer screens for each product we sell, so it's hard to remember what information goes where. It changes for each policy.

29

Step 1: Defining the Problem

After talking with her team, Jesse could see that there was more than one cause for her group's slow performance. She would keep this in mind as she continued to define her problem.

> **Take a Moment**
>
> Look back at your original problem and subject it to a Five-Why review:
>
> _____
> _____
> _____
> _____
> _____

Considering a Problem from Multiple Perspectives

Identifying your problem and its causes is an important first step toward defining it, but your analysis shouldn't stop there. When Dr. Jonas Salk was asked how he discovered the vaccine that cured polio, he cryptically replied, "I learned to think as Mother Nature thinks." His answer points out the importance of considering a problem from a variety of perspectives.

Who Is Affected by the Problem?

Unless your problem is small, you are probably not the only person affected by it. Identifying other people with a stake in the problem and considering how they would describe it encourages you to generate the most useful definition possible. Questions like these help you broaden your perspective on the problem:

- Who is affected by this problem?

- How would these people describe the problem?

- How would their description differ from mine?

Unless your problem is small, you are probably not the only person affected by it.

Step 1: Defining the Problem

Continue to change perspectives until you consider everyone affected. Then confirm your characterizations by talking to the people themselves. If other perspectives on the problem are very different from yours, you may want to restate your earlier description of the problem.

To see how this type of perspective-taking works, let's return to Jesse's case study.

■ Whose perspectives should Jesse consider as she tries to solve her work problem? Jesse began by listing everyone she could think of who was affected by the situation. She asked how they would characterize the problem. She began to see that several groups of people were affected by the problem and that each group would describe it in a different way. Her list included:

- **Policyholders:** define the problem as having to fill out difficult forms and wait too long for reimbursements.

- **Customer service:** defines the problem as a high volume of complaints about difficult forms and the long waiting period.

- **Management:** defines the problem as a loss of business revenue when dissatisfied policyholders switch to other insurance companies.

- **Claims processors:** believe they are working as fast as they can and define the problem as unreasonable expectations on the part of policyholders and management.

Once she completed her list, Jesse took time to talk to a representative of each group. She began to see that her earlier statement of the problem, "My work team isn't completing its assignments quickly enough," didn't fully describe the situation.

● **Step 1: Defining the Problem**

> **Take a Moment**
>
> Now return to your problem—the one you identified earlier. Are other people affected by it? List those people on the lines at the left below. Would their definitions of the problem agree with yours? Determine what their definitions would be and write them in the lines to the right of the names.
>
> _____ _____
>
> _____ _____
>
> _____ _____
>
> _____ _____
>
> _____ _____

What Other Perspectives Should You Consider?

To broaden your perspective further, try thinking about the problem from the perspective of someone totally unrelated to it. Whose perspectives you should consider? Try asking yourself the following questions:

Try thinking about the problem from the perspective of someone totally unrelated to it.

- Who else might have useful thoughts or opinions about this problem?

- How would they describe the problem?

- How would their descriptions differ from mine and the descriptions of those affected?

An expert, or someone who has had experience with a similar type of problem, can provide you with useful insights, but don't stop there. Sometimes, a perspective that seems totally unrelated to the problem at hand can give you exactly the inspiration you're looking for. How would a child or a clown describe your problem? an artist or a minister? a politician or, as in Dr. Jonas

Step 1: Defining the Problem

Salk's case, Mother Nature herself? Try to put yourself in others' shoes. If possible, talk directly with some of these people and record their thoughts in their own words.

The more perspectives on a problem you can gather, the more accurate your final definition of that problem will be. By taking a variety of viewpoints into account, you will be able to see aspects of a problem you may have initially missed. This will increase the insights you are able to bring to the next step of problem solving: generating a solution.

> ### Take a Moment
> Think of the problem you identified earlier. Is there an expert whose perspective might provide you with some useful insights? What other perspectives might help you to see the problem in a new way?
>
> _____
>
> _____
>
> _____

Creating a Working Definition of the Problem

Once you identify your problem and its root causes and consider the problem from a variety of perspectives, you're ready to create a working definition of the problem. Your working definition is important because it provides the focus for solutions you generate in the next step of the problem-solving process.

To create a working definition of your problem, review your initial statement of the problem and the other perspectives you considered.

Your working definition provides the focus for solutions you generate in the next step of the problem-solving process.

- Now that you've had a chance to consider other perspectives, does your initial statement still accurately reflect the problem?

33

Step 1: Defining the Problem

- Based on the other perspectives, how would you change your description of the problem?

- Based on everything you learned during this stage of the problem-solving process, write a new statement of your problem.

Our case study illustrates how the use of multiple perspectives might cause you to change the definition of a problem.

Case Study

■ After reviewing her own description of her work team's problem and the perspectives of others involved in the situation, Jesse decided that the root cause of everyone's complaints seemed to be the claims process itself. If it could run more efficiently, everyone's problems would be solved. Jesse decided to rephrase her statement of the problem from "My work team isn't completing its assignments quickly enough" to "How can we make claims processing move more efficiently?"

Chapter Summary

We can look at the problem-solving process as a cycle that consists of the following steps:

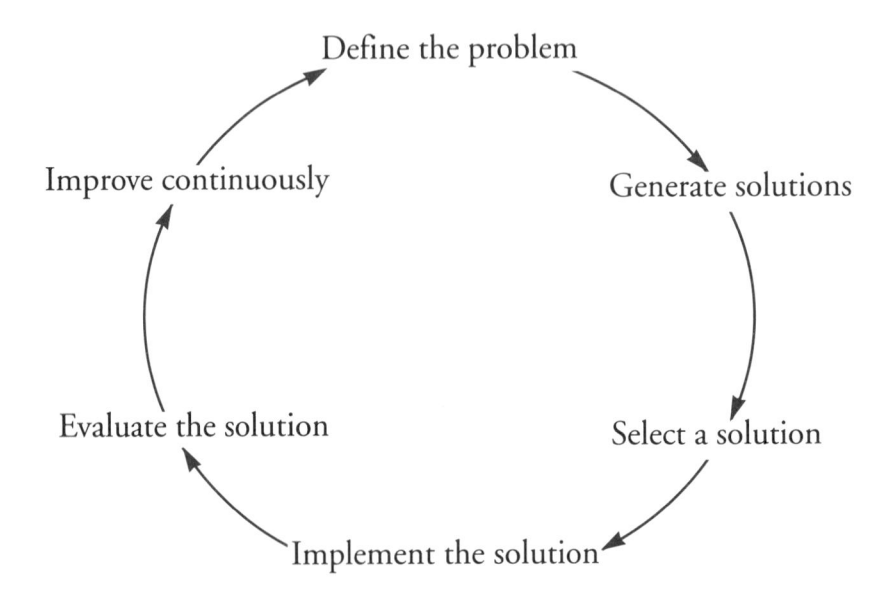

Define the problem → Generate solutions → Select a solution → Implement the solution → Evaluate the solution → Improve continuously → (back to Define the problem)

Step 1: Defining the Problem

We will have the most success in developing effective solutions if we approach the problem-solving process with a positive attitude. We can do this by thinking of our problems as interesting challenges and opportunities for greater achievement.

Before we begin the problem-solving process, we should decide how much time we want to devote to a particular problem. We should base our decision on the problem's overall importance and allocate at least half of our time to identifying and describing the problem.

We can solve a problem most effectively when we have a clear definition of it. Many times this involves identifying smaller problems that work together to create a complex situation. We can identify the problems involved by asking ourselves a series of questions, such as:

- What are possible causes of this situation?
- Which of these causes are problems in themselves?
- What concerns surround these problems?
- What aspects of this situation are not actual problems?

We can examine our problems visually by using a Fishbone Diagram to set out major categories of problems and the individual problems behind them. We can identify the root causes of our problems by using the Five-Why Technique, which involves asking a series of *why* questions.

Once we identify a problem, we should consider it from other perspectives. We should consider perspectives of other people who might be affected by the problem, as well as those of people unaffected by the problem who might give us new insights. We should take these perspectives into account as we create a working definition of the problem that helps us focus our problem-solving efforts.

Step 1: Defining the Problem

Self-Check: Chapter 2 Review

Answer the questions below. Suggested answers appear on page 120 and 121.

1. How can we bring a positive perspective to problem solving?

   _____
   _____
   _____

2. How should you determine how much time to devote to solving a problem?

   _____
   _____
   _____

3. List four questions that can help you identify underlying problems within a complex situation.

   a. _____

   b. _____

   c. _____

   d. _____

4. Describe the Five-Why Technique.

   _____
   _____
   _____

Step 1: Defining the Problem

5. Why is it important to consider different perspectives when solving a problem?

   _____

   _____

   _____

● **Step 2: Generating Solutions**

Chapter *Three*

Step 2: Generating Solutions

> ### Chapter Objectives
> ▶ Recognize your own creativity.
> ▶ Brainstorm for problem solutions.
> ▶ Use the Janusian Technique to see opposite sides of a problem.
> ▶ Synthesize ideas from diverse fields to gain new insights into a problem.
> ▶ Create metaphors to place problems in new contexts.
> ▶ Use the Full-Circle Method to generate new ideas about a problem.

With a clear definition of your problem in mind, you're ready to take the second step of the problem-solving process: generating solutions. This part of the process calls for innovation and spontaneity as you turn your creative side loose on the problem. Focus your efforts on generating as many potential solutions as possible. As literary critic Mark Van Doren observed, "Bring ideas in and entertain them royally. One of them may be the king." During the next step of the process, you'll have the opportunity to determine which solutions are most workable.

Unleashing Your Creativity

Despite the assertions of some people that they don't have a creative bone in their bodies, the truth is we are all born with the capacity for creativity. Unfortunately, some of us saw our early imaginative efforts ridiculed, so we stopped tapping into our creative selves.

Step 2: Generating Solutions

The results of this criticism are seen in one famous study of creativity that tested the same children on the same test questions at ages 5, 10, 15, and when they were in college. At age 5, 92 percent of the students were found to be "very creative." By age 10, that figure had dropped to 37 percent. By age 15, only 12 percent of the children were deemed "very creative." Sadly, by college, the number of "very creative" children was only 2 percent.

The good news is that we can easily recapture our creativity if we are willing to exert some effort. There are several techniques that can help you tap into your creativity. They include:

- Brainstorming for solutions
- Using the Janusian Technique
- Synthesizing ideas from diverse fields
- Thinking metaphorically
- Using the Full-Circle Method

> **The good news is that we can easily recapture our creativity if we are willing to exert some effort.**

Brainstorming for Solutions

In most problem-solving situations, the first step to generating solutions is to brainstorm. *Brainstorming,* a simple technique that can be done individually or in a group, consists of three basic steps:

1. Write down your definition of the problem to be solved. If you are working in a group, write the problem on something large, like a dry-erase board or a pad on an easel, so everyone can see it. If you are working alone, scratch paper will do.

2. For the next several minutes, write down as many solutions to the problem as possible. If you are facilitating a group, write solutions on the dry-erase board as members of the group call them out. The most important point to remember in this part of the process is to let your imagination go. Write down any solution without judging it, no matter how unusual or unworkable it may sound.

● Step 2: Generating Solutions

3. Keep writing solutions as long as you or your group members continue to generate ideas. If suggestions from group members appear to be tapering off, bring the session to a close by asking for final thoughts. In the next step of the problem-solving process, you will have the opportunity to evaluate the solutions you just generated.

If you are working with people who are particularly shy or reluctant to talk, you might try giving members a few minutes of quiet time to collect their thoughts after you introduce the problem in Step 1. Then begin Step 2 by asking group members to share what they've written. This should break the ice and open the door to more spontaneous comments.

Take a Moment

Write down a problem you've been trying to solve.

_____

_____

Now, either working alone or with a group, brainstorm some possible solutions. Let your imagination go. You can worry later about how practical your ideas are.

_____

_____

_____

_____

_____

Step 2: Generating Solutions

Using the Janusian Technique to See Opposite Sides of a Problem

Although simple brainstorming can be very effective, it may not give you the number or variety of solutions you want, especially if you are working alone. Luckily, other idea-generating techniques can help you jump-start your creativity. A method that works especially well for generating solutions is the *Janusian Technique,* named after Janus, the ancient Roman god of beginnings and endings. Janus appears on Roman coins with two profiles looking in opposite directions, and the thought process named after him also requires you to think in opposite directions. Doing so frees you from mental constraints and allows you to think "outside the box."

> The Janusian Technique requires you to think in opposite directions.

The first step of the Janusian Technique involves asking yourself a series of questions related to the nature of your problem, including:

- Who could most likely solve the problem?
- How have similar problems been solved before?
- What process is usually used to resolve such problems?
- What tools are usually used to solve problems like this?

The second part of the Janusian Technique involves identifying the opposite of those answers:

- Who could *least* likely solve the problem?
- How have similar problems *not* been solved before?
- What process has *not* been used to resolve such problems?
- What tools have *not* been used to solve problems like this?

We can see how the Janusian Technique works by returning to Jesse's case study.

● Step 2: Generating Solutions

Case Study

- Jesse asked herself the following questions about her problem: "How can we make our work move more quickly?"

  - **Who could most likely solve the problem?**
    Employees processing claims.

  - **How have similar problems been solved before?**
    When goals in this company aren't met, management asks the employees to work harder or faster. This solution works for a while, but it is only temporary.

  - **What process is usually used to resolve such problems?**
    Management sends memos regarding the need to work faster; supervisors set new goals for employees.

  - **What tools are usually used to solve problems like this?**
    Incentives for meeting goals; public recognition.

  Jesse then began the second half of the Janusian technique by generating the opposite of her earlier answers. This took a little more effort because she had to imagine all of the possibilities that had never been tried.

  - **Who could *least* likely solve the problem?**
    Policyholders.

  - **How have similar problems *not* been solved before?**
    Management tried disciplining employees who don't meet goals, but this doesn't have much effect.

  - **What process has *not* been used to resolve such problems?**
    No one has ever reviewed work processes and claim forms to see if we are being as efficient as possible.

  - **What tools have *not* been used to solve problems like this?**
    Incentives have never been offered for new ideas about handling forms.

  As Jesse looked over her answers, she could see that there were many more ways to solve her problem than just asking her team to work faster.

Step 2: Generating Solutions

Take a Moment

Following Jesse's example, use the Janusian Technique to solve the problem you identified in the previous chapter, or some other problem facing you and/or your team.
Describe the problem:

_____

_____

Begin the first step of the Janusian Technique by answering the following questions:

- Who could most likely solve the problem?

  _____

- How have similar problems been solved before?

  _____

  _____

- What process is usually used to resolve such problems?

  _____

  _____

- What tools are usually used to solve problems like this?

  _____

  _____

Now, answer the questions from the *opposite* perspective:

- Who could *least* likely solve the problem?

  _____

Continued on next page

● **Step 2: Generating Solutions**

> **Take a Moment** *(continued)*
> - How have similar problems *not* been solved before?
>
>   _____
>   _____
>
> - What process has *not* been used to resolve such problems?
>
>   _____
>   _____
>
> - What tools have *not* been used to solve problems like this?
>
>   _____
>   _____
>
> Now, keeping in mind what you've written above, look for three unusual possible solutions for the problem you described.
>
> 1. _____
>
> 2. _____
>
> 3. _____

Synthesizing Ideas from Diverse Disciplines to Gain New Insights

Experts tell us that about a third of the reading we do should come from disciplines other than our own. Often, the fusion of unfamiliar concepts with familiar problems yields an unexpected source of ideas. For example, Harvard chemist Stuart Schreiber found he was able to distinguish male cockroaches from females by spraying a picogram (one-trillionth of a gram) of a chemical compound into the air. The male cockroaches immediately flapped their wings and stood up.

Step 2: Generating Solutions

What if you want to identify individuals in your organization with interest in volunteering for community service? What might make potential volunteers stand up and be counted? One approach could be visual: a picture of a lonely elderly person or a hungry child might touch the heartstrings of potential volunteers. Listing benefits of volunteering might be another way of showing how minimal effort can maximize return. Or, the endorsement of the company CEO might prompt some to become part of your team.

> ## Take a Moment
>
> Think of a problem you must solve within the next several weeks. After reading items from fields other than your own, formulate two possible solutions to the problem. This is not an easy task. Be ready to engage in mental aerobics!
>
> **State your problem:**
>
> _____
>
> _____
>
> **Facts from diverse disciplines:**
> - Scientists have discovered that we drop hot potatoes before we feel any pain, long before we have burned our hands. The reason? The moment you touch something hot, nerves relay a signal to the spinal cord which, in turn, forces you to drop the potato. The message doesn't even get to your brain. A reflex action causes your fingers to spread and the potato to drop.
>
> - The average person has about 50 quarts of water in his or her body. But the water is not pure H_2O. Rather, it is a saline solution. Some scientists believe the salt solution is a residual fluid from a time when all land animals lived in the sea. Because salt is lost in the liquid we perspire, people sometimes take salt pills to retain the needed balance.
>
> - In 1875, a train was lost in the quicksand of Colorado. Even though tracking efforts went as far down as 50 feet, the train was never located. *Quicksand* is layers of
>
> *Continued on next page*

● **Step 2: Generating Solutions**

Take a Moment *(continued)*

sand formed on sand flats that lie above clay. Because water cannot move through a clay base, it remains in the sand. The saturated mixture is a thick fluid that sucks anything heavy into itself.

- Pretzels can be traced back to the 7th century, when a monk in France looked at the folded arms of his fellow monks in prayer. This particular monk baked bread at the monastery and one day decided to twist the dough to resemble the praying form.

Possible solutions to your problem prompted by the preceding facts:

1. _____

   _____

2. _____

   _____

Creating Metaphors to Place Problems in New Contexts

A *metaphor* is a comparison between two things not usually compared.

The metaphor has been described as the most powerful force on Earth. Despite its simplicity—the *metaphor* is merely a comparison between two things not usually compared—it conveys some very complex ideas. To capture the restrictive, punitive nature of communism, for example, Winston Churchill referred to it as "the Iron Curtain." And to describe the invisible barriers that are sometimes used to keep certain groups from advancing professionally, Anne Morrison spoke of "the glass ceiling."

The well-expressed metaphor helps you generate solutions to a problem because it places the problem in a new context, creating new insights. Because your mind is required to regard new relationships, new images, and new expressions, the likelihood of your creating new solutions is greatly enhanced.

Step 2: Generating Solutions

In the world of business, metaphors abound. Here are a few examples:

- It's a jungle out there.
- The ball is in our court now.
- He marches to the beat of a different drummer.
- She's a pit bull when it comes to negotiating.

How do you create a metaphor for your problem? Follow these steps:

1. Identify a problem that will continue to cause tension until it is resolved.

2. Complete this statement: "This problem makes me think of _____." (Alternatives are: "This problem is like _____" or "This problem could be compared to _____.")

3. List features associated with the item to which you compared the problem in Step 2.

4. Review the list of features you created in Step 3. Choose one that sums up the problem for you. Ask yourself what solutions this feature suggests.

We can see how this process works by considering Jesse's case study again.

- When Jesse thought about her problem ("How can we make our work move more quickly?"), it reminded her of trying to run a race with lead weights tied around her feet. Some features she listed for Step 3 were:

    - The need to reach a goal
    - Trying to move quickly, but not being able to
    - Dragging something that keeps holding you back
    - Feeling that others are watching
    - Finishing last and feeling exhausted

● Step 2: Generating Solutions

As she looked at her list, Jesse decided that "Dragging something that keeps holding you back" summed up how she felt about claims processing. The solution her metaphor suggested? Find out what was slowing down her team's work process and eliminate it.

Using the Full-Circle Method to Generate New Ideas

Another means for generating solutions to problems is the *Full-Circle Method.* This method is based on a visual model: a circle divided into four quadrants, as illustrated below.

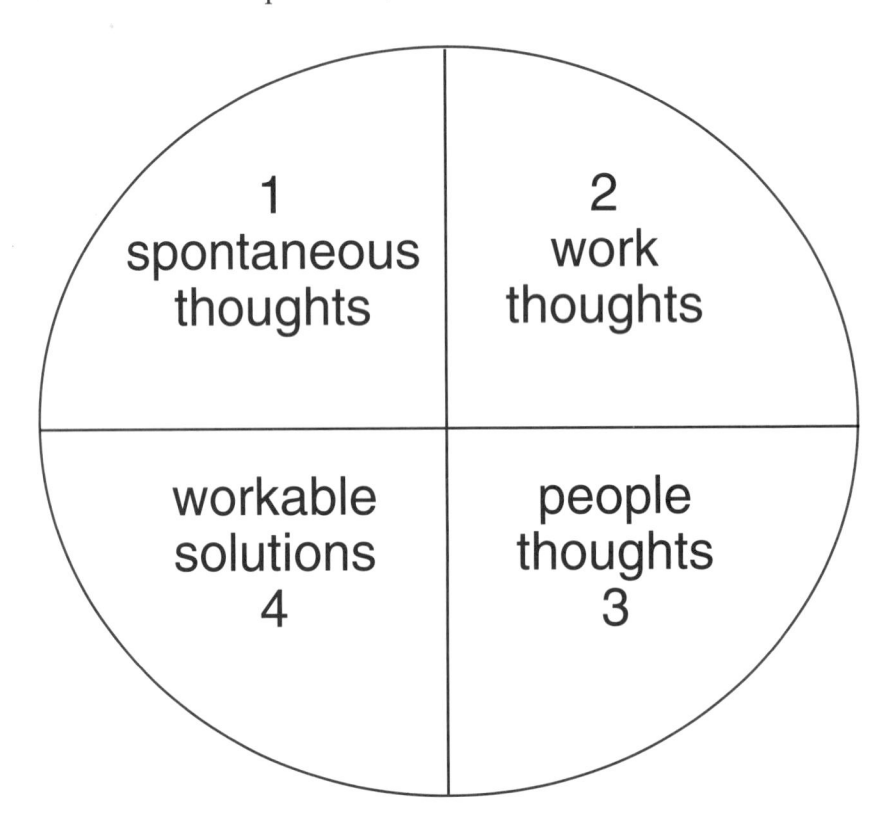

Each quadrant of the circle represents a step in the problem-solving process.

Each quadrant of the circle represents a step in the problem-solving process. To begin the process, identify a problem you need to solve and move to the first quadrant.

1. Begin with the upper left-hand quadrant: spontaneous thoughts. As quickly as you can, for three full minutes, write all the thoughts that are in your head, whether or not they relate to this problem. They will be random and maybe even strange. Record them anyway.

Step 2: Generating Solutions

2. Move to the second quadrant: work thoughts. For three minutes, with your mind focused on the problem you outlined, let ideas spill out regarding work. (Remember, you are not necessarily looking for solutions during the first three steps; concentrate on flexing your mental muscles.)

3. Move to the third quadrant: people thoughts. For three minutes, write down whatever thoughts are in your head as you juxtapose your problem with people. Think about coworkers, customers, suppliers, lawyers, teams, departments, anyone with whom you come in contact. As you do, jot down what is in your mind.

4. This step brings you "full circle" as you consider the last quadrant. For five to 10 minutes, look over your preceding lists and try to find workable solutions among the ideas presented in the first three steps.

Take a Moment

Use the Full-Circle Method to generate solutions for a problem facing you or your team.

Describe a problem you would like to solve.

_____

_____

Now, follow Steps 1 through 4 described earlier. List the solutions you generate below.

_____

_____

_____

_____

_____

_____

● **Step 2: Generating Solutions**

Chapter Summary

Although we may not think of ourselves as creative, each of us is capable of generating creative solutions to problems. Several techniques for idea generation help us tap into our creativity. These include:

- Brainstorming to generate as many solutions as possible.

- Using the Janusian Technique to see opposite sides of a problem.

- Synthesizing ideas from diverse disciplines to gain new insights into a problem.

- Creating metaphors to help place problems in a new context.

- Using the Full-Circle Method to generate new ideas for problem solving.

One or more of these methods will help you identify a variety of potential solutions to most types of problems. In the next chapter, we'll discover some other ways that people who work in groups can generate solutions. We'll also consider how to work on problem solving in a team setting. While not an actual step in the problem-solving process, team skills are a vital part of solving work-related problems.

Step 2: Generating Solutions

Self-Check: Chapter 3 Review

Answer the questions below. Suggested answers appear on page 121.

1. True or False?
   Research shows that some people are creative and others simply are not.

2. True or False?
   Janusian refers to the process of interpersonal and collective deliberation.

3. True or False?
   About 50 percent of the time we spend reading should be spent reading about things outside our field of interest.

4. List the steps involved in creating a metaphor for a problem.

   a. _____

   b. _____

   c. _____

   d. _____

5. List the four quadrants of the Full-Circle Method.

   a. _____

   b. _____

   c. _____

   d. _____

• **Working with Teams**

Chapter *Four*

Working with Teams

> **Chapter Objectives**
>
> ▶ Model the traits and behaviors of successful problem-solving teams.
>
> ▶ Identify and apply techniques used by high-performance teams when they meet.
>
> ▶ Distinguish between task and maintenance behaviors needed in team settings.
>
> ▶ Employ at least two consensus tools, as individuals or teams, to choose between alternatives.

A popular saying observes, "If you're not part of the solution, you're part of the problem." In the workplace, problem-solving teams work continuously to improve quality, customer service, processes, and cycle times. But if teams do not function cooperatively, they actually become the problem. In fact, the inability to work together guarantees problems will not be solved and compounds the original problem by creating tension, alienation, and wasted effort.

Regard this chapter as an insert—it does not discuss the next step in the problem-solving cycle. However, many of the problems you face involve collaborative efforts with coworkers, so we feel it is important to briefly step out of sequence at this point. So far, we have studied how to:

1. Define the problem.

2. Generate solutions.

We will examine how effective teams function before we continue with how to

3. Select a solution.

Working with Teams

4. Implement the solution.

5. Evaluate the solution.

6. Improve continuously.

Characteristics of Successful Teams

Without understanding the dynamics of successful teams and the causes of dysfunction in teams, you and your colleagues will have a difficult time completing the problem-solving sequence.

Successful teams are characterized by respect and appreciation among team members as well as a commitment to the team's mission and each other. How do they achieve this state? They begin at the beginning. To sharpen your skills at identifying what works and what doesn't work when forming teams, we present a case study based on a workplace situation.

> **Successful teams are characterized by respect and appreciation among team members.**

Case Study

■ A health care organization assembled a focus group to study customer satisfaction. Because the resulting feedback was very negative, management asked Roberto, the team leader, to solve the problem(s). Roberto called his team together for their first meeting.

As you read Roberto's opening remarks, make a note of problems (those not related to the problem of customer dissatisfaction) you believe this team is facing or will soon encounter.

> I've selected you to be on my team—all 15 of you—because management is quite concerned with the results of the focus group. As you know, the focus group was assembled to assess the level of satisfaction that patients and their families feel about the care we provide. Their feedback indicates that satisfaction levels are low. Management wants us to do something about raising those levels. We all work in Admissions. We all know each other. We should be able to figure this out. Any ideas?

Working with Teams

> **Take a Moment**
>
> What problems do you find in Roberto's introduction?
>
> _____
>
> _____
>
> _____

Read through the following categories of problems to learn how many you spotted in Roberto's remarks. Although he only spoke one 30-second paragraph, Roberto planted the seeds for numerous difficulties to sprout later.

Team Makeup

Ideally, people agree to participate on teams instead of being forced or manipulated into serving on them.

Ideally, people agree to participate on teams instead of being forced or manipulated into serving on them. Roberto probably appointed his whole department to the team instead of asking who wished to be part of it and/or determining who needed to be part of it. Author and educator Will Schutz advises team leaders to ask two questions that may initially sound scornful. In reality, though, these two questions help us find the right people to serve on the team. The questions are: *Who knows?* and *Who cares?*

To answer the *Who knows?* question, select individuals who are truly knowledgeable about the process to be improved or the problem to be solved. In Roberto's case, if the majority of patient complaints concern Emergency Room treatment, a team from the Admissions Office would not have much to offer regarding improvements in ER treatment.

As for *Who cares?* consider that people who are passionately committed to streamlining a given process or reducing the waste associated with it may bring invaluable resources to the team, although they may not know as much as others with more experience or training. When Roberto reveals he "selected" team members, we are led to believe people did not volunteer, which means they are probably not the people most knowledgeable and/or most committed to the mission.

Working with Teams

Usually the department manager should not serve as team leader. The position of authority Roberto holds as a supervisor may interfere with members' willingness to speak openly. Team members may also fear offering opposing points of view or may agree with Roberto's viewpoint simply because it is politically correct to do so.

The size of Roberto's team is not ideal: 15 is an unwieldy number. Research by Robert Sternberg at Yale University shows that the best-functioning teams have about eight members. Professor Sternberg also studied the types of people who constitute the most productive teams. As proponents of cultural diversity know, the richest contributions come from people who do not all think alike, sound alike, look alike, and/or act alike. In our case study example, over the years, people from the Admissions Office have probably developed a similarity of outlook, procedures, and problem-solving methods that can hinder the development of innovative solutions.

> The best-functioning teams have about eight members.

The Yale studies found that every team needs at least one person who is logical and at least one person who is creative—information that parallels the emphases throughout this book on both convergent and divergent thinking. In addition, successful problem-solving teams include at least one person who is knowledgeable about the process in question, the kind of person Will Schutz seeks when he asks, *Who knows?*

> Every team needs at least one person who is logical and at least one person who is creative.

Because Roberto's health care organization wants to improve its overall level of customer satisfaction, and because complaints run across a number of departments, Roberto's team members should represent various departments. Of course, it is comfortable to work with people we have known for a while, and yet, Roberto's mission is to solve a problem, not to surround himself with people he knows well. Team leaders should select team members on the basis of what they can contribute to solving the problem, not on the basis of how long they have known each other and/or the leader.

● **Working with Teams**

Mission

Although Roberto alludes to the mission behind the team's formation, he does not make the mission clear. Nor does he offer clarity regarding expectations. Instead, Roberto jumps in and asks, "Any ideas?" without setting the framework within which good ideas could be generated. Team members need more information before they can begin to make suggestions.

> **Effective leaders send out an agenda before calling the first meeting.**

Effective leaders send out an agenda before calling the first meeting. At the top of the agenda, the team's mission is clearly articulated. Ideally, an attachment would be included so team members could see exactly what types of complaints patients and their families had, how frequently specific complaints occurred, and what one or two areas constitute the priorities on which team efforts will concentrate.

Introductions

Although the people on Roberto's team "know each other well," they really only know about one another's work in the Admissions Office. They probably know very little about each other's lives outside the Admissions Office. By spending a few minutes on an icebreaker activity before asking for ideas, Roberto can help relax team members and help them gain insights into each other's experiences. Here is what Roberto might have said:

Case Study

■ I realize we all know each other well, but the problem of poor customer satisfaction is a new one for us. It is not like Admissions problems we have solved in the past. So, we will need some fresh ideas, some new perspectives—even some solutions that are not common or ordinary for us. Let's take a few minutes to learn a little more about ourselves. We're all typical customers—customers who go to restaurants and hotels and hospitals and shopping centers. Choose one person to be your partner and discuss these two questions: In terms of being a customer, what "lights your fire," so to speak? And, as a customer, what "burns you up"?

This short exercise helps the team identify with patients who served on the focus group. It also helps develop an understanding of the dissatisfaction patients expressed. Sometimes, the exercise even allows solutions to bubble up as team members discuss with their partners what might have been done in the service encounters they described.

Working with Teams

Details

Especially at the first meeting, team members come filled with questions. The most proficient team leaders anticipate and address the majority of those questions, which include such concerns as:

- What are we supposed to do?
- How long will it take?
- To what degree are we empowered to do what has to be done?
- What deadlines are we facing?
- What resources are available?
- Whose approval do we need?
- How often will we meet?
- What happens if we fail?
- What happens if we succeed?
- What takes priority—this team's work or the work back on my desk?

Allow time for questions the leader has not anticipated. Before team members can work comfortably together and feel ready to take action, they must gain confidence. Confidence relates to team members' ability to solve the problem and their willingness to commit resources, especially time, to the task before them.

Setting the Tone

Roberto seems to regard low satisfaction levels as a thorn in the Admissions Department's collective side rather than an opportunity to excel. He implies that the team has assembled because "management wants something done" rather than because the hospital and staff are interested in improving services to patients. Additionally, when Roberto says, "we should be able to figure something out," he sets a tone of getting something done instead of thoroughly researching the problem and implementing the optimal solution.

> Before team members can work comfortably together and feel ready to take action, they must gain confidence.

Working with Teams

> To bring out the best in people, we must recognize the best in people.

To bring out the best in people, we must recognize the best in people. Team leaders especially need to exhibit a positive attitude to inspire team members. Roberto might emphasize the pride most employees take in their work, the hospital's long tradition of good service to the community, the importance of remaining competitive so everyone can continue to have jobs. He might also cite the critical need for quality in an industry that deals with life-and-death issues.

Techniques Used by High-Performance Teams

As we've mentioned, before the meeting begins, effective teams establish an agenda of items to think about and set time limits for each agenda item. Efforts made at the first meeting set the mood for subsequent work sessions. Introductions are made, questions are answered, concerns are aired, and the team's mission is made absolutely clear.

More formal techniques are employed by high-performance teams. Try to pinpoint what they are as you listen to a much-improved Roberto conduct a meeting in a manner more conducive to success than his first attempt.

- Thank you for being so prompt in arriving. It's good to see the ground rules we agreed to are being followed. Susan, will you be the topic monitor today? Joe, the time monitor? Thanks. And Tim, will you be the recorder? As you can tell from the agenda, we are going to discuss conducting a customer satisfaction survey. That should take about 20 minutes. We'll brainstorm ideas for the format of that survey and then determine how we want to proceed.

Take a Moment

What portions of this new introduction do you think work effectively? Why?

_____
_____
_____

Working with Teams

Recognition

Roberto complimented the group for their adherence to the ground rules, subtly reinforcing behaviors that enable team members to function cohesively. He acknowledged their professionalism and, indirectly, their dedication to the mission.

Ground Rules

Successful teams establish norms by which they agree to conduct their operations. These rules may pertain to procedural issues, such as how votes are taken. They may pertain to behavioral issues, such as allowing a member to speak without interruption. And they may pertain to commitment issues, such as following through on assigned tasks. The ground rules are often posted in the meeting room so the leader can refer to them as necessary.

Monitors

Even before the meeting got underway, Roberto appointed both a topic monitor to keep the discussion on track and a time monitor to ensure progress is made within the designated meeting period. Making such appointments at the beginning of every meeting will help each one run smoothly.

Most of the time, team leaders are too busy conducting the meeting to simultaneously serve as the recorder. Appoint another person to record the minutes of the meeting and the ideas generated during brainstorming sessions.

Combining Task and Maintenance Behaviors

In a sense, task and maintenance behaviors parallel the problem-solving styles of convergent and divergent thinking. When we focus on the tasks necessary to solve a problem, we move in a logical progression toward its solution. We are converging. Yet, if we are so focused that we neglect the social behaviors that help people work harmoniously, we may actually be slowing down that process.

Maintenance behaviors represent the interpersonal "glue" that brings about cohesion and cooperation. They require thinking that is more creative than analytical. When the improved Roberto, for example, suggests that the team engage in the

Task and maintenance behaviors parallel the problem-solving styles of convergent and divergent thinking.

Working with Teams

"What-lights-your-fire/What-burns-you-up?" icebreaker, he helps create team cohesiveness and a feeling of belonging for each member.

Study the following dialogue from the meeting Roberto conducted. Identify which behaviors represent task functions and which represent maintenance functions.

Case Study

Roberto:
What can we do to ensure the survey is filled out by our customers?

Terry:
I only fill out surveys if they're easy to read. If they're really long or complicated, I toss them out.

Roberto:
I can appreciate that. Tim, let's write "easy to use" on the flip chart. What else?

Lateisha:
I went to Slim Pickings yesterday. You know, that new restaurant down on Orchard. They serve lots of food to dieters. But it's all delicious. I've never tasted food that was so delicious. And—believe it or not—you can get a crabmeat melt on rye that has only 11 grams of fat. We're all . . .

Susan:
Excuse me, Lateisha, but we're getting off the topic here. Did they have a survey there for customers?

Lateisha:
Sorry. Yes, they did. It was a simple card. But when you turned it in at the cash register, they gave you a lollipop—fat-free, of course—to thank you for filling it out. So, I think we should figure out some way to thank our customers for taking the time to fill out the form.

Roberto:
Great. So far, Tim has two things down for us to consider. We need more. Sam, we haven't heard from you yet. Any thoughts?

Working with Teams

> ### Take a Moment
> Which statements in the dialogue on the previous page represent task functions? Which represent maintenance functions?
>
> _____
>
> _____
>
> _____

Even this brief look at the meeting in progress shows us several behaviors in each category. A number of task behaviors moved the group closer to a solution. When Roberto asked his first question, he was *initiating*. When he asked another question, he was *seeking information*. When Susan reminded Lateisha that she was going off track, she was *monitoring* the topic. And when Terry and Lateisha gave their examples, they were *participating* and *offering alternatives*. As Roberto checked with Tim to be sure the points were recorded, he was *overseeing* the meeting process. All of these are task behaviors—they keep us on target; they move us toward the accomplishment of a goal. Other task behaviors include *clarifying, summarizing, helping to reach consensus, monitoring time,* and *reminding the team of its purpose.*

When Roberto thanked participants for their ideas, he was *expressing appreciation,* and when he sought input from Sam, he was *encouraging*. Both of these are maintenance behaviors. Again, these behaviors make meetings run more smoothly because they fulfill members' psychological and physical needs. Additional maintenance behaviors include *harmonizing, compromising, recognizing, admonishing, involving each member, intervening when necessary,* and *identifying areas of agreement and disagreement.*

Identifying areas of agreement and disagreement ultimately leads to compromise, as the team arrives at an acceptable decision. The resulting decision may not represent everyone's favorite choice, but it's a choice with which everyone can live. We call this process *achieving consensus*.

● **Working with Teams**

Consensus Tools Used by Teams

Consensus may be achieved informally or formally. The process often requires team leaders with considerable skill at negotiation because enough options must be offered so that compromises can be made. The following question demonstrates informal consensus: "If we changed the word 'directions' to 'direction,' would you consider the passage acceptable?" At other times, the consensus process is more formal, following an established set of guidelines. Two of the more formal consensus tools follow.

Consensus Tool 1: Weighted Voting

The *Weighted Voting* method may be used by individuals or teams. "Weights" are assigned to the criteria you consider important, as we can see in the following case study.

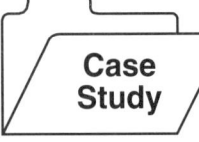

Case Study

■ You are a member of a personnel committee interviewing for a new secretary. As you prepare to interview job candidates, you determine which features of a good secretary are most important to you. Then you assign a weight to each feature to indicate its level of importance. Your weights run from 1 (less important) to 5 (very important):

Typing speed	5
Pleasant personality	4
Good communication skills	5
References	5
Familiarity with software programs	2

Your second step is to interview job candidates and determine how they fit the criteria listed above. Candidate 1 types 100 words per minute with only 2 errors, has a nice but rather reserved personality, completed one year of college (English major), has excellent references, and is familiar with basic word processing. Again, using a scale of 1 to 5 (1=lowest; 5=highest), you score her on the features you established earlier:

Typing speed	5
Pleasant personality	3
Good communication skills	4
References	5
Familiarity with software programs	3

Working with Teams

Next, you multiply Candidate 1's scores by the weights you originally established for each feature. You then add the results of that multiplication to determine a total score:

Typing speed	5 x 5 = 25
Pleasant personality	3 x 4 = 12
Good communication skills	4 x 5 = 20
References	5 x 5 = 25
Familiarity with software programs	3 x 2 = 6
TOTAL SCORE: 88	

You repeat the process for each candidate. The candidate with the highest total score is the one you should hire because the total score represents the level of importance you assigned to each feature.

For teams, proceed with Weighted Voting in the following manner. Give each team member three adhesive circles. Each circle is numbered either 1, 2, or 3. Members decide which three items on a displayed list are their top three choices. One at a time, members stick their adhesive circles on the listed items of their choice, giving the "3" circle to their favorite or most-liked option and the "1" to the least-favored. (It helps to equate the "3" with three pounds or three dollars, for example.) Once all team members identify their preferences, the team leader tallies the numbers and reveals the collective choice.

Consensus Tool 2: Nominal Group Technique

The second consensus tool, as its name implies, is used by teams to reduce the list of options under consideration. The Nominal Group Technique derives its name from the fact that the team functions as a team only in the nominal sense of the word. More emphasis is placed on individual preference than on collective choices. Individual preferences, though, will ultimately yield the team's course of action. This tool is especially useful for clarifying tough issues with which the team may be grappling. Team members begin the process by:

- Preparing a list of problems.

- Appointing a recorder and setting up two flip charts, if possible.

Working with Teams

The process then follows these steps:

1. **Select a problem.**
   The team selects one problem to examine thoroughly, and the recorder writes the problem in a full sentence on the flip chart. (Roberto's team, for example, might write this statement: "Customer satisfaction levels are unacceptably low.") Individual team members also write the statement from the flip chart onto their papers.

2. **Share responses to the problem.**
   A team facilitator or leader asks a volunteer to share his or her thoughts regarding the problem while the recorder writes them on the second flip chart. The facilitator then asks if anyone has a similar idea or related thought. This second comment is added to the flip chart. Each person is asked to contribute but can pass if he or she chooses. Round-robin sharing continues as long as team members have something to say. (Those who chose to pass on the first round are encouraged to present their ideas on subsequent rounds.) All responses are written on the flip chart. They are not, however, analyzed, probed, or discussed. Once all ideas are listed, the recorder labels them alphabetically.

3. **Clarify ideas.**
   Team members may now ask for clarification on any comments listed. The team leader encourages members to question the meaning of items on the chart and also tries to keep discussion open and flowing. In this stage, the leader's role is important: to ensure that ideas are amplified but not attacked, explored but not yet evaluated, expanded upon but not judged. It is important to maintain a neutral, inquiring atmosphere.

4. **Rank ideas.**
   The leader gives each person five 3 x 5 cards. In silence, team members choose the five items that represent their top priorities or favorite choices. They write one idea or code letter on each card, using a scale where 5 equals top priority and 1 equals lowest priority. All 3 x 5 cards are collected and rankings for each item are written on the flip chart. Obtain scores by multiplying each ranking by the number of times

it was chosen and then adding the totals for each item. The item with the highest score is the one on which the team should concentrate.

Note: All four steps of the process can be repeated several times. The final selection of a problem with its possible solution may not be made until numerous options have been explored.

> ## Take a Moment
> Are you currently involved in any team problem-solving situations in which you could use Weighted Voting or the Nominal Group Technique? Describe them.
>
> _____
>
> _____
>
> _____
>
> _____

Chapter Summary

Chapter 4 permitted us to step outside the problem-solving process temporarily and examine how to work in teams most efficiently. To be sure, the problem-solving process can and should be used by you alone. But, with the majority of American firms establishing teams, we all need to learn how to apply the problem-solving process in a group setting.

As we listened to Roberto's first efforts at meeting with a team, we discovered what not to do when we tackle problems. Roberto's team did not have the correct *composition*. Nor were they made aware of their *mission*. No time was spent on *introductions*. And *questions* that members probably had were never addressed. Roberto failed to set the *proper tone* for the meeting. In so doing, he lost an opportunity to develop interest in and commitment to the task at hand.

When we considered techniques used by high-performance teams, we found Roberto improved upon his initial overture.

Working with Teams

The second time around, he set an *agenda,* he *recognized* team members, he ensured *ground rules* were followed, and he appointed *monitors* to keep the meeting on schedule.

The next time we looked in on the meeting, we found Roberto and others employing various task and maintenance behaviors. *Task behaviors* echo the nature of convergent thinking in that they emphasize a sequential and deliberate movement toward task accomplishment. *Maintenance behaviors,* by comparison, deal more with creative and emotional aspects of our thinking and acting. When we are concerned about team members' comfort or wish to develop harmonious relationships, then we engage in behaviors that maintain interpersonal bonds. Little can be accomplished without such bonding.

In the next chapter, we continue the problem-solving cycle by examining the very deliberate process of selecting a solution. Called the Comparative Valuation Process, this detailed procedure helps determine the popularity, optimal use, and worth of each item being considered.

Working with Teams

Self-Check: Chapter 4 Review

Match the listed terms with the appropriate descriptions below, and write the corresponding letter in the blank at the right. Answers appear on page 122.

1. Nominal Group Technique _____
2. Task behaviors _____
3. Weighted Voting _____
4. Ground rules _____
5. Maintenance behaviors _____
6. Monitors _____

a. A means of achieving consensus by establishing criteria and assessing the merit of a given person or thing in relation to those criteria
b. A means of clarifying and ranking ideas
c. Interactions designed to ensure harmony among group members
d. Individuals selected to intervene when team members neglect to conform to agreed-upon rules
e. Agreed-upon behaviors to which members are expected to adhere
f. Actions designed to keep the meeting process moving

• **Step 3: Selecting a Solution**

Chapter *Five*

Step 3: Selecting a Solution

> **Chapter Objectives**
> ▶ Use an Affinity Diagram.
> ▶ Use the Comparative Valuation Process to select a solution.
> ▶ Think "outside the box."
> ▶ Consider consequences when selecting a solution.

Now that we've seen how teams can work together, it's time to return to the steps of the problem-solving process. Previously we saw how to develop our ideas so that we could complete Step 2, generating solutions to our problem. Now it's time for Step 3, selecting a solution from the many alternatives we developed through brainstorming or some other idea-generating activity. The more alternatives we have to choose from, the better. Excellent solutions evolve from multiple choices. In time, however, we must reduce choices, make decisions, and take action.

In the previous chapter, we discovered two easy-to-use strategies for narrowing choices: Weighted Voting and the Nominal Group Technique. By using numbers to make weighted selections, these techniques almost seem to make our choices for us. Such strategies work best when options or criteria are well-defined or well-focused, as we saw when Weighted Voting was used to hire a new employee. The skills/traits needed for a job were listed and an applicant's knowledge/ability was compared to the list.

Not all situations, however, are so well-defined or so focused on a given set of criteria. How do we reduce our choices, select the best solution, and reach concurrence when circumstances are

Step 3: Selecting a Solution

not clear-cut? Two methods, the *Affinity Diagram* and the *Comparative Valuation Process,* are useful, and we will examine each in detail. Both strategies begin with brainstorming, during which ideas fly fast and furiously, and both help uncover useful solutions from alternatives that may initially seem preposterous or absurd. But developing an Affinity Diagram generally consumes less time than the Comparative Valuation Process, so you may find it easier to use for most situations.

Grouping Alternatives with the Affinity Diagram

We try to encourage wild-solution ideas during brainstorming because taming wild ideas is easier than making boring ones larger than life. But we still need to get a handle on the mass of information that results from brainstorming. With the Affinity Diagram, ideas show their relationship (affinity) to one another and fall into groupings that can help us develop effective solutions.

Follow these steps to use the Affinity Diagram in your own group problem solving:

1. Assemble your team (no more than eight members). Be sure to include people who are not alike in job experience, outlook, stake in the outcome, and so forth. Develop a clear and simple problem statement that also invites broad solutions.

2. Prepare for brainstorming by creating two sites where ideas will be written:

    • On a flip chart

    • On self-stick notes or 3 x 5 cards

3. Begin brainstorming. Each person who offers an idea is responsible for writing it in a complete sentence on a self-stick note or 3 x 5 card. A designated recorder writes the idea on the flip chart, which acts as the collective memory.

4. As ideas surface, place all self-stick notes on a wall or all 3 x 5 cards on a flat surface (table or floor) so everyone on the team can see them. Keep generating ideas as long as people have new or different items to add.

> With the Affinity Diagram, ideas show their relationship (affinity) to one another and fall into groupings that can help us develop effective solutions.

Step 3: Selecting a Solution

5. When the flow of ideas stops, the sorting and reducing process begins. Use another wall or additional floor/table space to designate four areas into which you will group notes/cards.

6. As team members silently review all ideas written on self-stick notes or 3 x 5 cards, common themes or *affinities* should become apparent. Maintaining silence, team members move the notes/cards into groupings that seem appropriate. If a team member does not feel a particular card belongs in a particular group, he or she simply moves it into another group.

7. Once the grouping process ends, team members generate headings for each collection of ideas. Headings must use more than a single word. The headings must be phrases or sentences that can stand alone and that reflect the essence of all the ideas in a group. Headings are not right or wrong. They simply represent subdivisions of the larger problem.

8. When the team believes the Affinity Diagram is complete, they can submit it to a final review to be sure they agree on the headings that have been generated. They can also ask for an external review by others outside the team.

■ In the last chapter, we met Roberto and his team, who were assembled to study the problem of customer dissatisfaction. Following is the list of ideas they generated as possible solutions to the problem.

1. Hold a fair
2. Make ourselves more visible
3. Have another focus group
4. Put out a survey
5. Each One/Reach One campaign
6. Put mission statement on stationery
7. Benchmark: compare ourselves to world-class organizations
8. Join a patient-appreciation consortium
9. Do more public service
10. Ask employees to spread the word
11. Show customers we appreciate them with token gifts
12. Write articles about what we are doing
13. Appear on local television programs
14. Go into schools

Step 3: Selecting a Solution

15. Print literature to be distributed
16. Read more; learn more about customer service
17. Start with the worst complaints
18. Have administrators visit patients to acquire direct input
19. Have employees wear customer-friendly name tags

Roberto's team placed their 3 x 5 cards into these final groupings.

1	2	3	4
Have another focus group	Put out a survey	Benchmark: compare ourselves to world-class organizations	Hold a fair
Each One/Reach One campaign	Put mission statement on stationery	Join a patient-appreciation consortium	Make ourselves more visible
Go into schools	Ask employees to spread the word	Read more about customer service	Do more public service
	Show appreciation with token gifts		Write articles about what we are doing
	Print/distribute literature		Appear on local TV programs
	Start with the worst complaints		
	Have administrators visit patients		
	Have employees wear name tags		

Take a Moment

Using a full phrase or sentence for your labels, what heading would you create for each group?

1. _____

2. _____

Continued on next page

Step 3: Selecting a Solution

> **Take a Moment** *(continued)*
>
> 3. _____
>
> 4. _____
>
> Again, headings are not right or wrong. They are meant to help us clarify the problem. Categories such as *Expand into the Community, Use Internal Resources, Use External Resources,* and *Advertise Our Excellence* permit us to get a better handle on how to solve the problem.

By allowing broad issues to be identified, the Affinity Diagram works best when no cut-and-dried answers are readily apparent.

Once headings are created, some teams might prioritize the four groups and zero in on the one needing the most attention or the one that would produce the best results. Other teams might regard the four areas as equally important, dividing them among members for further action.

By allowing broad issues to be identified, the Affinity Diagram works best when no cut-and-dried answers are readily apparent. While preventing us from being drowned in a sea of possibilities, it permits us to pursue wider solutions rather than being forced to choose only one.

Evaluating Major Issues with the Comparative Valuation Process

Like developing an Affinity Diagram, the process of Comparative Valuation begins with a wide array of choices. This process, though, yields a final choice after we execute numerous, careful steps. When we compare in this way, we examine each choice from a number of perspectives. As a result, the process takes quite a bit of time, whether used individually or in groups, and is not appropriate for the majority of decisions. However, when critically important paths must be pursued or when strategic plans must be developed, the Comparative Valuation Process is an excellent means of selecting a direction in which to move.

Comparative Valuation examines each choice from a number of perspectives.

The complete Comparative Valuation Process consists of three components:

♦ Popularity (P) Evaluation

Step 3: Selecting a Solution

- Optimization (O) Level Assessment
- Worth (W) Assessment

Together, these three components yield the P-O-W Analysis. Although many decision makers stop after completing a Popularity Evaluation, using the complete package (P-O-W) assists with major issues and life choices. Here are the steps for completing the P-O-W process:

Step 1: State the Problem and Brainstorm Possible Solutions

Comparative Valuation begins, as do other selection techniques, with a description of a significant problem you or your team are required to solve. After clearly stating the problem, brainstorm 20 to 25 possible solutions.

Step 2: Reduce the List to 10 Top Choices

Record your top 10 choices on the blanks of a form similar to the one shown (ignore the numbers at the right for now).

```
1. _____    1  1  1  1  1  1  1  1  1
                             2  3  4  5  6  7  8  9  10
2. _____       2  2  2  2  2  2  2  2
                                3  4  5  6  7  8  9  10
3. _____          3  3  3  3  3  3  3
                                   4  5  6  7  8  9  10
4. _____             4  4  4  4  4  4
                                      5  6  7  8  9  10
5. _____                5  5  5  5  5
                                         6  7  8  9  10
6. _____                   6  6  6  6
                                            7  8  9  10
7. _____                      7  7  7
                                               8  9  10
8. _____                         8  8
                                                  9  10
9. _____                            9
                                                     10
10. _____
```

73

● **Step 3: Selecting a Solution**

Step 3: Compare Each Choice to All the Other Choices

This step resembles the handshake puzzle on page 12. Just as each person shook hands with every other person, each choice in the Comparative Valuation Process is compared to every other choice.

Using the numbers to the right of each selection, compare each option to every other option. For example, as you compare #1 and #2, ask yourself, "If I could only select one of these two, which one would I select?" Circle one choice that has a slight edge over another choice. Continue by comparing #1 to #3 and circling your preference. Then compare #1 to #4, to #5, and so on. Ask yourself the same question each time.

Now, count how many times you circled each number as it appeared to the right of the choices and record the totals. How many times did you circle #1? #2? Write down the total. Do the same for each number. (To check your accuracy, the total of all of your numbers should add up to 45.)

If the team as a whole wishes to obtain the Popularity Rating of the 10 choices, add the number of times each person on your team voted for each issue and divide the totals by the number of team members. This simple analysis may surprise you with its answers. After it has been carefully compared to the other selections, the solution you initially feel most drawn to may not always be the solution that emerges as the preferred one. If time is short, the process may be ended once you obtain the Popularity Rating.

■ To see how this process works, let's examine how the CEO of Roberto's health care organization used it to determine how the organization should invest its resources. She began by brainstorming a long list of critical issues to be discussed at the next Board of Directors meeting. Then she listed her top 10 priorities for resource investment shown on the next page:

Step 3: Selecting a Solution

1. Customer Service   ① 1 ① ① ① 1 1 1 1
                             2 ③ 4 5 6 ⑦ ⑧ ⑨ ⑩

2. Outsourcing Benefits   ② 2 ② ② 2 ② 2 2
                             3 ④ 5 6 ⑦ 8 ⑨ ⑩

3. Indemnity Insurance   3 3 ③ ③ ③ 3 ③
                             ④ ⑤ 6 ⑦ 8 ⑨ 10

4. Ethical Issues   4 4 4 ④ 4 ④
                             ⑤ ⑥ ⑦ 8 ⑨ 10

5. Physician-Led Health Delivery Networks   5 5 ⑤ ⑤ ⑤
                                            ⑥ ⑦ 8 9 10

6. Quality   6 ⑥ 6 ⑥
                             ⑦ 8 ⑨ 10

7. Practice Guidelines   ⑦ ⑦ ⑦
                             8 9 10

8. Alternative Medicine   ⑧ ⑧
                             9 10

9. Partnerships/Coalitions   ⑨
                             10

10. Federal Regulations

The CEO may have been satisfied with a simple "popularity" rating, which yielded these numbers (total = 45):

#1—4 times, #2—4 times, #3—4 times, #4—4 times, #5—5 times; #6—4 times; #7—9 times; #8—3 times; #9—6 times; #10—2 times.

Clearly, the choice toward which the CEO gravitated most often was #7: "Practice Guidelines," and the process could end here. However, if the problem you and/or your team must solve is a one of considerable importance, it deserves the additional time and effort required to complete the full Comparative Valuation Process. Now that our CEO has obtained the Popularity Rating, it's time to determine the Optimization and Worth assessments.

● **Step 3: Selecting a Solution**

Step 4: Determine the Optimization Level for Each Possible Solution

Decide how well each choice is currently performing or being used, and assign a percentage that reflects your rating. For example, if one possible solution to an organizational morale problem is *training*, ask how satisfied you are with the training currently provided. If little or no training is offered, or if what's offered is not well received, then "training" as a viable solution would receive a low optimization score, perhaps 10 percent or 20 percent. On the other hand, if training programs in your organization are *optimized*, if they are effective and far-reaching, then *training* as a solution deserves to receive a high score, maybe 90 percent or even 100 percent.

■ To return to our previous example, our health care CEO assigned the following percentages to the 10 choices, reflecting the extent to which each issue was already being handled:

#1—10%;   #2—0%;   #3—70%;   #4—90%;   #5—30%;
#6—75%;   #7—80%;   #8—25%;   #9—85%;   #10—20%

Apparently, item #4 (Ethical Issues) and item #9 (Partnerships/Coalitions) are issues already being dealt with effectively.

Step 5: Determine the Worth Level for Each Option

Now, consider the *future worth* of the solution, not the existing use of the possible choice. How valuable could the choice be to the organization? How much merit might it have in terms of the organization's goals? If implemented, to what extent would this option pay off? What is the potential worth of each item? Use a scale of 1 (low) to 10 (high) and consider the future results that might evolve from concerted efforts made by a team dedicated to implementing each choice.

To illustrate, if two options to address a morale problem were *training* and *more socializing,* what would be the respective worth of each possibility? If you think of training as more valuable than socializing, you might rate it 9, while you rate socializing at 3. Now expand the ranking to each of your 10 top solutions identified in our previous steps. Thinking about

Step 3: Selecting a Solution

investment of resources, which of the 10 choices could have the greatest benefit to the organization? Rate each possibility on a scale of 1 to 10, reflecting your opinion of each item's benefit.

- For example, our CEO rated the ten choices as follows, revealing the potential worth of investing time and effort in each of these areas:

    #1—3 ;   #2—9;   #3—8;   #4—10;   #5—4;   #6—5;
    #7—6;   #8—2;   #9—8;   #10—7

    Even though the Popularity Rating found item #7 (Practice Guidelines) to be the favored choice, by examining the value, or worth ratings, a different item emerges in importance: #4 (Ethical Issues).

Thus far, we examined Popularity, Optimization, and Worth (P-O-W) ratings for just one person, the CEO attempting to determine which items to emphasize with the Board of Directors. Remember, though, the Comparative Valuation Process can also be used by teams. Teams need to record and average each score for both Optimization Level and Worth Level, as described in Step 6 and Step 7.

● Step 3: Selecting a Solution

Step 6: Average the Team's Optimization Percentages

Determine the total percentage and the average percentage for each of the 10 solutions. Begin by recording each participant's Optimization score for each solution on a chart like the one below (letters are substituted for team member names). Add all percentages and write the number in the *Total* column. To obtain the average score for each solution, divide the total by the number of team members. Write that score in the *Avg* column for each of the 10 solutions.

Optimization Percentages

Member:	A	B	C	D	E	F	Total	Avg
Solution #1	90	85	75	80	90	75	495	82.5
#2	60	50	70	55	65	65	365	60.8
#3	70	70	65	60	75	65	405	67.5
#4	50	60	55	65	50	55	335	55.8
#5	70	65	70	75	60	80	420	70
#6	10	20	15	20	15	15	95	15.8
#7	90	80	85	80	75	80	490	81.7
#8	70	75	70	65	65	65	410	68.3
#9	15	15	20	10	15	10	85	14.2
#10	80	90	95	80	80	85	510	85

Step 3: Selecting a Solution

Step 7: Average the Team's Worth Ratings

Repeat the process used to obtain the Optimization percentages. Determine total numbers and average ratings for each of the 10 solutions. Begin by recording each participant's Worth score for each solution on a chart like the one below. Tally all scores and write the number in the *Total* column. To obtain the average score for each solution, divide the total by the number of team members. Write that number in the *Avg* column.

Worth Percentages

Member:	A	B	C	D	E	F	Total	Avg
Solution #1	7	9	8	7	7	9	47	7.8
#2	6	9	5	6	7	6	39	6.5
#3	4	5	8	5	6	7	35	5.8
#4	2	2	6	4	2	5	21	3.5
#5	6	7	7	8	5	6	39	6.5
#6	8	9	8	8	9	7	49	8.2
#7	4	5	7	7	6	5	34	5.7
#8	3	6	6	7	5	4	31	5.2
#9	9	9	8	9	8	9	52	8.7
#10	8	7	5	7	6	8	41	6.8

Step 3: Selecting a Solution

Step 8: Plot the Values on a Grid

Using the averaged Optimization percentages and the averaged Worth ratings, plot the two sets of numbers on a grid. Indicate percentages for Optimization on the horizontal continuum. Indicate Worth ratings on the vertical continuum.

When you complete this step, you and/or your team may be tempted to latch on to the solution you believe is revealed by the grid, but it is critical that you take time to analyze results.

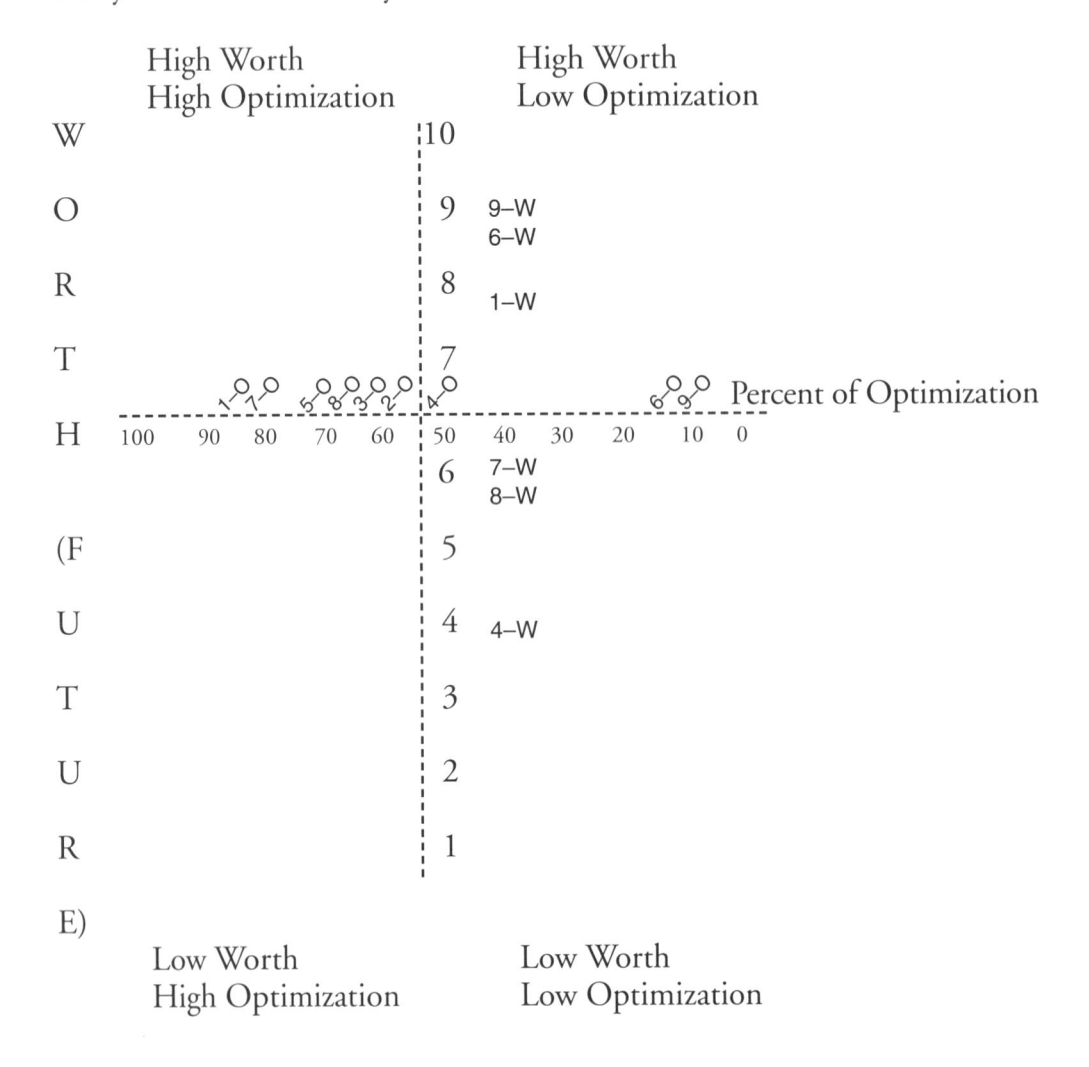

```
                High Worth              High Worth
                High Optimization       Low Optimization
    W
                                10
    O
                                 9    9–W
                                      6–W
    R
                                 8
                                      1–W
    T
            ○○○   ○○○○○ ○                ○○○
            1-7   5-8-3-2  4              6-9     Percent of Optimization
    H      100 90  80  70  60  50  40  30  20  10  0
                                 6    7–W
                                      8–W
   (F
                                 5
    U
                                 4    4–W
    T
                                 3
    U
                                 2
    R
                                 1
    E)
                Low Worth               Low Worth
                High Optimization       Low Optimization
```

80

Step 3: Selecting a Solution

Step 9: Analyze the Results

Contrary to what most people think, solutions with both high Optimization and high Worth are *not* the best to pursue. Solutions with high Worth but low Optimization are ones that will prove to be most advantageous for teams to undertake. If the solution is already being implemented, if its Optimization potential has already been tapped, it will not yield results as powerful as those found in solutions with low Optimization and high Worth.

Roberto's team, working on the same issues our CEO worked on alone, found that item #6 (Quality) and item #9 (Partnerships/Coalitions), when viewed from two additional perspectives, were most viable as solutions meriting further consideration. In truth, the Popularity Rating is the least important of the three criteria, and should influence decisions about the best course of action to pursue only if there is a tie between two issues in the upper right-hand quadrant.

The full Popularity-Optimization-Worth (P-O-W) Analysis of the Comparative Valuation Process does take time. But in the long run, it saves time and money by helping to ensure that scarce and ever-dwindling resources are not distributed over several choices and/or allocated to poor choices. When dealing with major issues, such as those involved in strategic planning, impacts on mission, or even life choices, such effort is warranted. As Cicero commented thousands of years ago, "The greater the difficulty, the greater the glory." The P-O-W Analysis often leads to "glorious" results for situations involving great difficulty.

Take a Moment

Are you currently involved in any problem-solving situations in which you could use Comparative Valuation? Describe them.

_____

_____

_____

Step 3: Selecting a Solution

Thinking "Outside the Box"

What if your problems are relatively simple problems that do not warrant the full-blown attention of processes such as the P-O-W Analysis? Sometimes we come across brainteasers or puzzles that test our ability to look at what everyone else is looking at while seeing what no one else can see (a popular definition of creativity). In order to select the best or most original solution, we need to come at the problem from a different perspective. At such times, we need to think divergently.

Consider the following diagram and answer the question: "Which letter does not belong?"

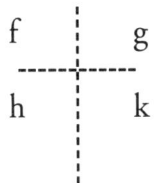

```
    f   |   g
  ------+------
    h   |   k
        |
```

What is your answer? _____

Why did you select it? _____

_____

_____

While many solutions are possible, the best answer is one that requires you to think *outside the box,* to step back and look at the whole picture instead of its individual parts. You'll find such a solution on page 122.

The ability to see outside the box depends upon your ability to understand the confines of the box and your determination to go beyond those confines. Let's look at two workplace scenarios which demonstrate how to achieve outside-the-box clarity.

Step 3: Selecting a Solution

To Train or Not to Train

■ Brian works in the training department of a large government agency. Recently, he received requests for training sessions that go beyond traditional offerings. Because the requests do not fall within approved training guidelines, Brian's first reaction is to deny the requests, knowing that funding is not available. When Brian acts on his initial impulse, he demonstrates "inside-the-box" thinking. Fortunately, Brian came up with a solution that benefits everyone involved. He began by listing his assumptions.

Case Study

Listed Assumptions:

1. If it's not on the approved list, it cannot be offered.
2. We have no instructors to teach such programs.
3. We need to pay for training.

Next, Brian examined those assumptions to determine their validity.

Validated Assumptions:

1. Brian checked to see if programs could be offered in a less-formal setting (lunchtime lectures or after-hours programs). He learned his manager had no problem with such a plan.

2. Brian began asking and learned that a number of employees, although not trained as instructors, had extensive knowledge in a variety of fields.

3. Brian considered the seemingly far-fetched idea of not paying instructors for their time. To his surprise, he learned that several people were willing to conduct classes at no charge.

Sorting the Mail

■ Maria is secretary to the principal of a small-town high school. The job demands a lot of her, but she prefers a fast pace to one that drags through the day. Part of her job requires that she sort each day's mail. Maria does not believe in the concept of "junk mail" because several glossy advertisements proved to be quite valuable to staff members. And yet, she finds the mail-sorting aspect of her job demands more and more time. Maria used "outside-the-box" thinking to alleviate

Case Study

Step 3: Selecting a Solution

the pressure placed upon her with each day's mail delivery. Her solution simultaneously brought "joy to the workplace," to use the words of quality master Dr. W. Edwards Deming.

Maria's technique was a simple one: she actually envisioned herself in a box and thought about how the box, symbolizing her job, could be made bigger (big enough to include the instructional staff). She stepped outside the narrow box that defined her job by seeing it as a much wider, more encompassing box. Maria asked herself this question: "Is it really necessary for me, and me alone, to do all this mail sorting each day?" After deciding it was not, she obtained approval from her principal to undertake the following project.

Every Monday morning, teachers are greeted with a banner as they walk into the front office. Though the names change each week, the ballooned and ribboned banner announces, "Congratulations, Mrs. Edison. You have been chosen this week's Junk Mail Manager." As part of the "ceremony," the principal shakes the hand of the appointed teacher (a different one is selected each week so no individual is overburdened) and thanks him or her for the generous gift of time. At the end of the week, the principal signs and delivers a thank-you note to the teacher who assumed the junk-mail task for that week.

Considering the Consequences of Your Actions

Several subprocesses exist within the problem-solving process. Selecting a solution, for example, has a smaller process all its own. As we saw in preceding case studies, once we step outside the box, we must still validate assumptions and/or obtain approval before we can begin to implement solutions. Although we discussed many things to consider regarding possible solutions to a problem, one final caution bears mentioning. Even after careful and deliberate selection of an option to pursue, individuals and teams should ask "What are the possible consequences of this action?" Sometimes, as we anticipate possible dangers or costs associated with a given course of action, we may decide it is not worth taking. Read the following case study and decide what you would do in a similar circumstance.

Step 3: Selecting a Solution

What's in the Dessert?

- Cynthia, a self-admitted perfectionist, worked very hard to arrange an outdoor banquet to honor visiting executives from the headquarters of a multinational firm. Everything went exactly as planned; even the weather cooperated. Guests mingled with their hosts in a relaxed but elegant setting. Serving dessert was the evening's final event, after which Cynthia could relax, knowing that months of planning culminated in an evening deserving of high praise. To her horror, though, Cynthia discovered that the dessert table had attracted ants. She immediately ran to the kitchen and, in a panic, begged the chef to prepare a new dessert. But clearly, it was too late for that.

    Case Study

    If you were in Cynthia's place, what would you have done?
    1. Explain what happened and apologize to the guests.
    2. Run to the nearest store and buy another dessert to serve.
    3. Serve the dessert anyway and, in the dim light, hope guests would not notice.
    4. Simply serve coffee as if you had planned for the evening to end without dessert.

    Cynthia chose solution 3, hoping that the darkness of evening would cover up the ant invasion. She also soaked some napkins with pesticide and placed them beneath the food trays in an effort to combat the insects.

    Consider for a moment the possible consequences of this unethical action. People could have become seriously ill from the pesticide fumes. Had anyone discovered the ants in the dessert, the evening would have been ruined anyway. And should anyone have discovered Cynthia's duplicity (for example, if the chef had revealed that Cynthia knew all along about bugs in the food but decided to serve it anyway), her reputation and possibly her career would have been ruined. In this case, Cynthia unwisely put her own desire for accolades and a flawless evening ahead of the welfare of her guests.

No matter what choice you made, now that you have had a chance to consider the consequences, do you agree with Cynthia's decision? Probably not. A useful and deceptively simple tool, that of considering the consequences of our actions, can help us determine correct choices.

Step 3: Selecting a Solution

Chapter Summary

The *Affinity Diagram* is a tool that enables us to quickly, if silently, manage a large amount of data by organizing it into related chunks. Once 3 x 5 cards are assembled in various categories and headings are prepared for each category, teams and individuals can more readily select solutions they feel will most benefit the organization.

Another valuable tool for selection is the *Comparative Valuation Process,* also useful to both individuals and teams. Because it's a lengthy process, it such should only be used with those issues that fall into the strategic-solutions area. From a list of 10 options, individuals or teams work through the Comparative Valuation Process on their way to isolating the most feasible solutions, as follows:

1. Obtain the Popularity (P) rating by comparing every solution to every other solution and totaling the number of times each solution is selected. Comparisons can stop here, but exploration of two other factors, Optimization and Worth, yield a full P-O-W Analysis.

2. Obtain the Optimization (O) level for each solution by writing a percentage to reflect the extent to which the option is currently being used.

3. Obtain the Worth (W) rating for each solution by ascribing a number from 1 (low) to 10 (high) to show the value each option could have, if implemented.

4. If the team is using the P-O-W Analysis, determine the average percentages from the Optimization scores.

5. Determine the team's average Worth ratings.

6. Plot values for both Optimization and Worth on a grid.

7. Analyze results: items falling into the High Worth/Low Optimization quadrant yield the best return on investments of time and money. Other elements of the final analysis include determining which of several items in a category should be worked on first, what resources are available for various solutions in a quadrant, and so forth.

Step 3: Selecting a Solution

Problem solving is expedited when we keep an open mind to possibilities, not only those springing from our own thought processes, but also possibilities offered by others in team settings. Flex your mental muscles and think "outside-the-box" by *listing assumptions* and *validating assumptions*. Often, we find our assumptions are based on opinion and not on unalterable facts. Another way to expand your thinking is to imagine a bigger "box," one that includes unusual (for the box) people, places, and/or things.

Throughout various stages of problem solving, we should ask questions that help us explore possible consequences of selected actions. Ask "What if?" questions and "So what?" questions, callous as they may initially sound.

However we arrive at a point, we must begin implementing our choice. In our next chapter, we'll learn more about putting our choices to work, at work.

Step 3: Selecting a Solution

Self-Check: Chapter 5 Review

Imagine yourself teaching a coworker to use the Comparative Valuation Process. In the space below, describe the elements of this tool, which begin with a brief description of the problem to be solved, followed by a brainstormed list of 20 to 25 alternatives.

1. Think about the P-O-W Analysis. First, identify what the letters mean:

    P = _____

    O = _____

    W = _____

2. Next, describe the remaining steps.

    a. _____

    b. _____

    c. _____

    d. _____

    e. _____

    f. _____

    g. _____

    h. _____

    i. _____

    Once you feel your explanation is clear, check your answers by turning to page 122.

● **Step 4: Implementing the Solution**

Chapter *Six*

Implementing the Solution

> ### Chapter Objectives
> ▶ Apply Lewin's Change Model for overcoming resistance to change.
>
> ▶ Use the 5-X Strategy to implement your solution.

Some people believe that the process of solving a problem is easier to execute than the process of putting the solution to work. Although the first process requires several steps (define the problem, generate ideas, and select a solution) and the second involves only one (implement the solution), the second can be difficult because it involves change.

In 500 B.C., Heraclitus observed, "The only permanent thing is change." Change results each time we generate a new solution to a problem. Even if the solution is one that has been implemented before, the present circumstances are different from the earlier ones. The speed of change in our society is illustrated by this quote from a Putnam Investments advertisement for mutual funds: "You may think you understand the situation, but what you don't understand is that the situation has just changed."

Some people think they can bury their heads in the sand and ignore change until it goes away. What they don't realize, of course, is that while they are waiting with their heads buried, they are exposing the most vulnerable part of their anatomy. And during that exposure, change is certain to occur anyway.

You can help these people overcome their resistance to change and effectively implement your solution with the help of two techniques: *Lewin's Change Model* and the *5X Strategy*.

Step 4: Implementing the Solution

Overcoming Resistance with Lewin's Change Model

As psychologist Kurt Lewin observes, people need to be introduced to change before change is introduced. This wording may initially sound confusing, but it actually sums up an important fact about how you should treat the change that any new solution can bring.

Just as you would introduce two people who do not know each other, you need to make others aware of your proposed solution and the effect it will have on them before you attempt to implement that solution. In this way, people will be more likely to accept your solution and adopt it as their usual practice. Lewin compares this process to melting ice and sums it up in three steps:

1. **Melt**
   Prepare the people who will be most affected by the change, melting the resistance of those who are frozen in their ways. Explain the change thoroughly, emphasizing the benefits it will have for those involved in the situation. Be ready to answer questions and relieve people's anxieties. The goal of this stage is to get others to open their minds a bit wider and accept a different way of doing things.

2. **Change**
   When you sense that resistance has melted, you can begin to implement the change itself. Be sure to collect data about the situation in question before, during, and after the change is introduced. This will help you determine if the solution you have chosen has improved the situation. As the saying goes, "If you can't count it, it doesn't count." Another saying reminds us, "Without backup data, you're just another person with an opinion."

3. **Solidify**
   If the change created by your solution improves the situation, take measures to solidify the new process. This means encouraging those involved to adopt it as the accepted way of doing things. Your solution has a better chance of being sustained over time if it receives full acceptance. When the solution is institutionalized, the time and effort that have gone into it are maximized.

> **Prepare the people who will be most affected by the change.**

● Step 4: Implementing the Solution

The following case study illustrates the process:

Case Study

■ Jee is an exhibits manager who, in the past, has had a somewhat adversarial relationship with the sales department. She has decided to solve the problem by resolving the conflict. To begin, she wants to bring warmth to the "cold war" that exists between the two departments. She intends to melt the existing enmity between them by exploring what has gone wrong in the past. At the first meeting (at which she has beverages and snacks available), she discusses an important trade show that will be held in two months.

Keeping the sales-driven mission in the forefront, she explains that she hopes they will sell more of their products in their exhibits there than they have ever sold before. Next, Jee acknowledges the problems that have plagued collaboration between the two departments before. Citing the tremendous opportunity offered by the upcoming show, she opens the floor to a discussion of past difficulties.

Every two weeks, Jee brings the sales and exhibits departments together. Then, two weeks before the trade show, she introduces the change she believes will positively impact sales: she has obtained approval to have two sales retirees attend the conference. Not only are they two of the best salespeople the company has ever known, they have agreed to help out for the cost of travel expenses alone. What's more, they have indicated an interest in "rejoining the team" on a regular basis. At this and subsequent meetings, Jee works out the details with the regular salespeople. She works to incorporate their recommendations from earlier discussions into the plans for this trade show.

In order to freeze this new policy into place, Jee has done a number of things: she has brought the two retirees into the planning meetings, and she has written a memo detailing the ways they might assist at the conference. What else could Jee do to solidify this new policy of having retirees work at future trade shows?

_____

_____

Step 4: Implementing the Solution

Of course, with the passage of time and the advent of new technology, or even new leadership, the changes that have been wrought by a given solution may be replaced by a new solution. Then, the three-step process begins all over.

Take a Moment

In order to gain some practice with this Change Model, outline quickly a problem that now exists in your workplace or a situation that you feel should be improved:

_____

_____

What is one possible solution to the problem?

_____

_____

Next, tell what existing mind-sets would have to be melted down in order for the solution you have in mind to be accepted. What attitudes would have to change if others are going to adopt the new way of doing things?

_____

_____

_____

_____

_____

Continued on next page

● **Step 4: Implementing the Solution**

> **Take a Moment** (*continued*)
>
> Assume you have managed to effect a change-receptive environment. How would you go about implementing the solution you believe is the best way to solve the problem or improve the situation? Briefly outline a plan here.
>
> _____
> _____
> _____
> _____
>
> Finally, what measures would you undertake to ensure the change will be maintained? How would you refreeze attitudes so that the solution you have introduced becomes the standard operating procedure?
>
> _____
> _____
> _____
> _____

Implementing Solutions with the 5-X Strategy

Another useful model for introducing change is the 5-X Strategy. It offers five easy-to-remember steps that will help you overcome resistance and gain acceptance for your solution.

1. **EXpect**
   Anticipate the reluctance others will have, especially in the beginning, as you present your proposed solution. Sometimes you have to work in spite of their opposition—as evident in the popular saying, "Those who say it can't be done should get out of the way of those who are doing it." However, it is undeniably better to have the resisters on your side.

Step 4: Implementing the Solution

One way to win them over is to be prepared for the comments you will hear. Have your verbal ammunition ready to offset the negativity you are bound to encounter. The more precedents you can cite, the more statistics you can garner to prove the solution's worth, the better your chances of gaining followers.

2. **EXamine**
In this step, you will consider all the people, places, and things that will be impacted by the proposed solution. Those individuals who are suppliers to or customers of your work process must be taken into consideration. So must more abstract things like budgets, timelines, politics, and morale. Spend most of your time on this step—examining possible pitfalls now will prevent you from tumbling into them later.

3. **EXplain**
Effective persuaders understand the power of the WIFM ("What's In It For Me?") Factor. To increase the likelihood of full support for your proposal, it will be necessary to explain to all affected parties the merits of your solution. Explore these benefits on both an individual and an organizational level. Cite the advantages for both the present and the future.

Admittedly, the present benefits may be more difficult to cite because payoff does not occur until the future. Nonetheless, an observation similar to the following would set the stage for future benefits by specifying a present one:

> ■ I've called you together regarding our policy of preparing monthly variance reports. They take time, I know, and I'm aware of your complaints regarding them. Well, I have good news. You don't have to do them any longer—at least not by hand. We've purchased new software that allows us to do them electronically. Yes, you will have to learn the programs, but once you've had the training, you'll find your preparation time sliced in half—I guarantee!

Step 4: Implementing the Solution

4. **EXecute**
    After careful planning and preparing, you are ready to put your plan into action. Part of that action, to be sure, is the gathering of facts that will allow you to gauge the effectiveness of the solution you have chosen. Pre- and post-intervention data permit us to make decisions regarding the solution: should it be extended as is, modified, or abandoned altogether?

5. **EXtend**
    Assuming you decide the solution is effective enough to be continued, you owe it to yourself and to your employer to take steps for extending the plan. Extending it over a longer period of time, perhaps, or extending it for wider usage or to a larger group of employees. It is certainly possible that extending might mean publicizing the success of the solution—through trade journals or professional conferences—so others might benefit from your solution. Extending could even mean forming new alliances—with other industries, with community agencies, with schools, etc.—so that the solution that has worked well in limited circumstances could be extended to embrace new scenarios.

The following example shows how one employee put the 5-X Strategy into action:

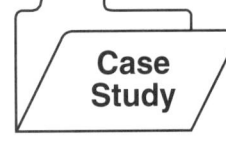

Case Study

■ Patrick functions in a culture of empowerment. About two weeks ago, he proposed the idea of a new "trademark" to his manager. The trademark he designed combines visual and verbal elements and reflects the company's new emphasis on Total Quality principles. The manager agreed that it was time for a new focus and asked only that he have a chance to see it before Patrick began using it in lieu of their previous symbol. Patrick is now ready to share the symbol with customers.

He expects there will be questions about why they are no longer using the old symbol, which stressed pride and professionalism but did not mention quality—a thrust that has become all-important in Patrick's company. A short letter, showing the new trademark, examines what improved quality means to customers and specifies what the company is doing to "build quality in."

Patrick goes on to explain the quality award the company has recently received. He discusses the meaning behind the new

Step 4: Implementing the Solution

symbol and how this new emphasis will benefit customers. The letter also points out some new quality initiatives being executed. In order to serve customers better, the letter notes, customer feedback is being solicited so the effect of improvement efforts can be measured. Patrick concludes by extending to customers an invitation to participate in those feedback mechanisms via focus groups and customer surveys.

Note: If the proposed solution is for a problem of a personal rather than work-related nature, you would follow the very same steps. You know yourself. You know what excuses you are likely to give or what resistance you can expect from yourself. You must also, as part of your strategy, remind yourself of the benefits that will accrue if you are faithful to the plan you have determined to be a workable solution to an identified problem. Further, you must examine who and what will be affected by your proposed solution.

If you decided the solution to "getting your life together" or "improving your health" was a diet, then with the third step, you would take into account changing your eating habits, or buying different kinds of food, or establishing a support system with people you can count on. The fourth step, of course, has you actually beginning the diet, and the final step asks you to think about ways of extending these healthful actions for the rest of your life.

Take a Moment

Identify a solution you would like to implement using the 5-X Strategy. What would you do to implement the solution at each of the five steps?

1. _____

2. _____

3. _____

4. _____

5. _____

Step 4: Implementing the Solution

Chapter Summary

Simple as it appears on the surface, Kurt Lewin's Change Model can prevent complex problems from developing further down the road. There are only three steps to this model:

1. Melt
2. Change
3. Solidify

It is the first stage that many solution implementers overlook as they work to effect improvements based on solutions they have reached. If we do not take time to thaw the attitudes and behaviors that have been frozen into rigid patterns over time, we have little hope of achieving the results we desire. The change should not be foisted upon others—no matter how beneficial that change might be—until they have had an opportunity to acclimate themselves to it.

Once the change has been introduced, we work to institutionalize it, to make it standard operating procedure—fully cognizant of the fact that, in time, this change may be changed again.

The 5-X Strategy also benefits solution implementers by asking them to:

1. Expect resistance.
2. Examine who/what will be impacted by the change.
3. Examine the benefits that will accrue to the various people/places/things affected.
4. Execute the plan.
5. Extend its success.

In the next chapter, we will consider various means of evaluating the solution so we can best determine if and exactly how the success of a given solution should be extended.

Step 4: Implementing the Solution

Self-Check: Chapter 6 Review

Answer the questions below. Suggested answers appear on page 123.

1. Kurt Lewin's Change Model contains three steps. What are they?

    a. _____

    b. _____

    c. _____

2. What are the five "X" words in the 5-X Strategy, and what does each mean in terms of implementing a solution?

    EX_____

    _____

    EX_____

    _____

    EX_____

    _____

    EX_____

    _____

    EX_____

    _____

● **Step 5: Evaluating the Solution**

Chapter *Seven*

Step 5: Evaluating the Solution

> ### Chapter Objectives
> ▶ Track the results of your selected solution.
>
> ▶ Work with individuals who can assist with interpretation.
>
> ▶ Find creative alternatives for calibrating the executed solution.
>
> ▶ Take advantage of lessons learned.
>
> ▶ Employ the P-D-C-A Cycle for problem solving.

Once we determine the success of a selected solution, the next step is to extend that success. If we implement a solution on a trial basis and it turns out to be successful, we can extend the solution by making it permanent. Or, if our solution works well in a given setting, we might extend it to other settings, other departments, divisions, or organizations. But the *if* is a big one. We need to spend considerable time and energy evaluating our efforts before we apply them on a wider basis. In this chapter, we'll consider several means of evaluation.

Tracking Results

The way in which you track the results of a solution depends on the type of solution you are implementing. If your solution involves comparing numerical amounts, such as the frequency of errors before and after the solution is implemented, you will take a *quantitative* approach to your evaluation. This involves gathering statistics and other numerical information. If your solution involves changing people's attitudes or opinions, you will take a *qualitative* approach. This involves asking others how they define the quality of a given experience.

If your solution involves comparing numerical amounts, you will take a quantitative approach. If your solution involves changing people's attitudes or opinions, you will take a qualitative approach.

Step 5: Evaluating the Solution

Taking a Quantitative Approach: The Correlation Chart

One easy-to-use quantitative tool is the *correlation chart,* which depicts the *correlation relationship* between two variables. While the correlation chart does not prove that one event causes another (a *causal relationship*), it does suggest links that can be explored further. Correlation charts are of greatest value when links between two variables are not definite and you need to discover what the connection might be, as in the following example.

The correlation chart suggests links that can be explored further.

- Vincentia is a public safety officer who was asked to track motor vehicle accidents in her community. When she used a correlation chart to examine the relationship between the number of accidents and days of the week, she discovered that Fridays had the highest level of accidents. Her chart looked like this:

Number of Motor Vehicle Accidents

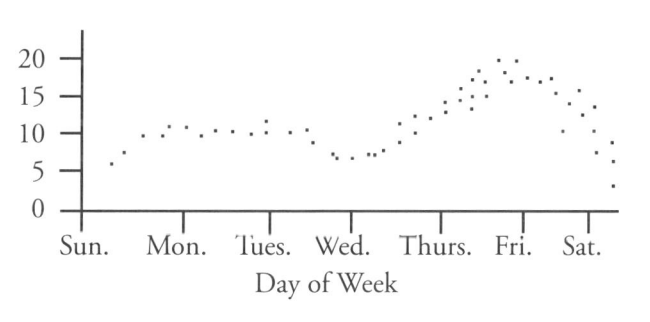

Vincentia's chart did not prove that Fridays themselves caused more traffic accidents. However, based on this correlation, Vincentia began to look at other types of behaviors that occurred on Friday. She discovered that after receiving their Friday paychecks, many people stopped at local taverns and consumed more than their usual amount of alcohol.

Believing that alcohol could be a factor in the accidents, Vincentia enlisted the help of tavern owners to provide free soft drinks for designated drivers and to call cabs for customers who appeared unable to drive. When she did a second correlation chart after these changes were made, she saw that the accident levels on Fridays now more closely resembled those for other days of the week.

Step 5: Evaluating the Solution

> ## Take a Moment
>
> Make your own correlation chart by following these simple steps:
>
> 1. Select one variable—the factor you hope to improve through control or change.
>
> 2. Select a second variable that you suspect is related to the first.
>
> 3. Collect about 75 pairs of data for both variables. In the example on the previous page, a note was made every time an accident occurred. The day of the week when the accident occurred was also recorded. These two items of information constitute one pair of data.
>
> 4. Draw a chart depicting the first variable on the X, or horizontal axis and the second variable on the Y, or vertical axis.
>
> 5. Plot each data pair as one point.
>
> 6. If you think several possible factors may be related to your first variable, prepare correlation charts for each. By comparing the charts, you should be able to tell which factors are related.

Taking a Qualitative Approach: The Focus Group

If the solution you are implementing involves changing people's opinions rather than numerical frequencies, you will need to evaluate it with a *qualitative* approach. When we evaluate qualitatively, we gather opinions. In other words, we speak to people, actively soliciting both positive and negative input.

Soliciting feedback is one example of qualitative evaluation. After we implement a solution, we can ask those affected by it how successful they believe it is. Such input gives us a sense of the big picture, without which we may be tempted to look at results from a narrow perspective, distorting our impression of overall success. If a product launches on time, within budget, and with more media attention than expected, we deserve to claim a certain degree of success. However, if customers do not like the new product, the success picture changes.

Step 5: Evaluating the Solution

A more formal means of gathering feedback from those affected by a change is the *focus group*. This involves gathering people into groups and asking for their feedback in a structured setting. Focus groups can be fairly easy to conduct if you follow these steps:

1. Assemble a group of six or seven people who are connected in some way to the implemented solution.

2. Ask permission of all in attendance to tape-record the session. Regardless of your note-taking speed, both verbal and nonverbal points will be lost as ideas are discussed.

3. The session should be structured yet flexible. Structure is found in a prepared agenda that covers the most important points and asks the most critical questions. Flexibility comes in the form of a relaxed atmosphere where people feel free to respond frankly.

4. As members of the group share impressions, put your ego aside. The group was not assembled so that you could solicit praise or defend your actions. Rather, you have asked for their valuable time to provide information that is critical to evaluating the success of your solution. Therefore, you must listen. Often, you are better able to listen when an independent facilitator leads the focus group session as you and your team sit inconspicuously to the side, saving questions and comments for the end of the meeting.

5. Plan with your team to meet immediately after the session, while information and impressions are fresh. Plan also to meet a week later, after you've had an opportunity to reflect on what you've learned.

If you are pleased with insights provided by your focus group, you may want to assemble others in the future. Use them to evaluate solutions that will have a far-reaching impact. You might ask the group for input before the intervention has been implemented and again after it has been put into effect. In this way, you have qualitative data to compare.

> **Focus groups allow you to gather people together and ask for their feedback in a structured setting.**

Step 5: Evaluating the Solution

Take a Moment

Think of a solution you and/or your team recently implemented. What results have you tracked regarding the effectiveness of this solution? Record them here:

_____

_____

_____

Next, list the names of six or seven people whose input would enable you to better understand your solution relative to the big picture.

1. _____

2. _____

3. _____

4. _____

5. _____

6. _____

7. _____

What neutral third party could facilitate a focus session?

_____

How would you structure the agenda? What topics should be covered in order to fully understand the context within which the solution was implemented?

_____

_____

_____

Step 5: Evaluating the Solution

Fine-Tuning Your Solution

After all the data are in and the picture is as big as possible, you must make decisions regarding the effectiveness of the selected solution:

1. Should you let the solution stand and rely on it with increasing frequency in the future?

2. Should you reject the solution altogether and select another to pursue?

3. Should you retain the solution but modify the approach?

Even if you and/or your team decides to abandon the solution completely and pursue another alternative, you should still ask if there is anything in the current solution worth salvaging. Is there any part of the strategy that could be replicated, although the approach as a whole is not one you would choose in the future?

If the solution was generally effective but needed minor adjustments, use these guidelines to aid you in fine-tuning the process.

1. Break down the solution and the implementation strategy into smaller, sequential steps.

2. Determine which steps were mildly successful and which were wildly successful. Maintain those elements as the core of your revised implementation.

3. Determine the causes of failure for the unsuccessful steps. Did they take too long? Cost too much? Did you fail to "melt" or "thaw" before introducing the strategy? Was appropriate approval obtained? Do attitudes need to be adjusted? Was proper equipment available? Ask these and other questions to determine what needs modification.

> **Determine the causes of failure for the unsuccessful steps.**

4. Make necessary changes. Changes may include changing dimensions (making something longer, shorter, thicker, etc.); changing aspects of time or distance; or adding, subtracting, or combining different items. Track the results of your changes to ensure no further adjustments are needed.

● Step 5: Evaluating the Solution

Take a Moment
Review the following case study and ask yourself how you would fine-tune the solution if you were in Calvin's situation.

■ Calvin is a relatively new member of the sales team in a large software company. As such, he feels he is not gaining the respect and recognition he deserves. Recently, he read that one way to increase his visibility is to send his boss copies of documents he has prepared along with copies of pertinent journal and newspaper articles.

Initially, Calvin thought this was the perfect solution to his problem because his boss thanked him for a particularly relevant article on user testing of software documentation. Just yesterday, though, Calvin's boss confessed to suffering from "information overload" and asked Calvin to stop sending him so much reading matter.

If you were Calvin, would you:
a. Continue to forward material, despite the boss' request?
b. Stop sending material altogether?
c. Fine-tune the approach and send only occasional but vital pieces?

Of course, answers may vary depending on the personality of the boss, but in this instance, fine-tuning seems the most viable alternative, especially because at first the boss was grateful for having received the information. Choose wisely and, in all likelihood, the boss will appreciate your judicious selection.

Compiling the Lessons You've Learned

Once you've implemented a solution and studied the results, compile a list of the lessons you've learned to help you with your next problem-solving project. Among questions you and/or your team should answer are these:

♦ If we were to do this again, what would we do differently?

♦ What would we not do the next time?

Step 5: Evaluating the Solution

- What did we fail to plan for?
- Where did we waste time?
- Whom would we consult the next time?
- Who profited most from this solution?
- What liaisons proved important?
- What did we learn?
- What was an unexpected benefit?
- What barriers did we have to surmount? Which proved insurmountable?
- How well did we communicate our intentions?
- How can we sustain the efforts already expended?

Following the Steps of the P-D-C-A Cycle

So far, we have discussed a number of techniques for identifying a problem, generating and selecting solutions to that problem, implementing those solutions, and evaluating our results. An easy-to-remember model that summarizes the steps of this problem-solving process is the *Plan-Do-Check-Act* or *P-D-C-A Cycle* originated by Dr. Walter Shewhart and used by business-people throughout the world.

1. **Plan**—Study the situation and plan your solution.

2. **Do**—Put the solution into effect.

3. **Check**—Monitor implementation and continually track results.

4. **Act**—Once data are analyzed, action is taken either to modify the solution, institute it wholeheartedly, or abandon it altogether.

On the next page is a case study that shows the steps of the P-D-C-A Cycle in action.

● Step 5: Evaluating the Solution

Case Study

■ T. R. Johnstone heads a construction company that is building a new hotel in California. He oversees every aspect of the business and, although he has attorneys on retainer, he is aware of health care and litigation costs that could seriously impact his company. Mr. Johnstone recently charted the number of his employees'/subcontractors' sunstroke incidents and is determined that, in the new fiscal year, he will lower costs associated with those incidents. Here is his **Plan:**

1. Have a physician from the nearby hospital address employees on the danger of heat exhaustion at the beginning of the summer months.
2. Distribute written materials based on the physician's recommendations.
3. Make containers of juice and water available every day at every site.
4. Instruct supervisors to give workers two additional five-minute breaks each morning and each afternoon when the temperature rises above 80 degrees.

In the **Do** stage of the P-D-C-A Cycle, Mr. Johnstone executes the plan he worked out for the next summer season. As summer approaches, he advises employees and subcontractors of his concern for their safety and tells them he will conduct frequent **Checks** to ensure their safety and well-being. Based on results he obtains during and after the summer season, Mr. Johnstone **Acts** to implement the plan as developed, abandon it altogether and substitute one that works better, or continue with the basic plan after making some adjustments to it.

As you can see, following the P-D-C-A Cycle can help you complete the steps needed to make your problem-solving process a success.

Chapter Summary

Ignoring the evaluation stage of problem solving defeats its entire purpose. We must keep track of vital data in order to know if our solution solved our problem. To do this, we need to capture data that existed before our solution was put in place and compare them to data that exist after our solution was implemented.

Step 5: Evaluating the Solution

When we use a *quantitative* means of evaluating, we are depending on statistics or numerical frequencies. One type of quantitative evaluation, the *correlation chart*, helps us understand the relationship between the frequency of certain events and the likelihood that particular factors may be causing the frequency. These charts are especially useful if prepared both before and after the implementation of a given solution.

A second type of evaluation, *qualitative* reports, can also be valuable. To obtain this type of data, we need to work with others to learn their opinions about particular events or conditions. The *focus group* can provide insights not revealed in an examination of quantitative data alone.

In evaluating the effectiveness of our solutions to personal and/or professional problems, we need to use our creativity, our contacts, and our communication skills. If evaluation indicates the solution is basically sound but needs fine-tuning, we can make improvements in a number of ways.

We can successfully complete the steps of the problem-solving process by following Dr. Walter Shewhart's P-D-C-A Cycle.

1. Plan—Study the situation and plan your solution.

2. Do—Put the solution into effect.

3. Check—Monitor implementation and continually track results.

4. Act—Once data are analyzed, action is taken either to modify the solution, institute it wholeheartedly, or abandon it altogether.

As the P-D-C-A Cycle indicates, problem solving is an ongoing process that involves the constant review and reevaluation of solutions. In Chapter 8, we'll examine ways to keep the cycle going by making continuous improvement a way of life and a way of work.

● **Step 5: Evaluating the Solution**

Self-Check: Chapter 7 Review

Answer the questions below by circling the choice you believe best completes the sentence. Suggested answers appear on page 123.

1. *Quantitative data* refers to
   a. Large quantities of information systematically gathered.
   b. Data that are measured.
   c. Data collected for use in strategic decisions, such as downsizing.

2. A *correlation chart*
   a. Shows the relationship between two variables.
   b. Correlates to the organizational mission.
   c. Charts your progress in following the problem-solving steps.

3. *Qualitative data* refers to
   a. Ways to improve the quality of work processes.
   b. Information regarding the Total Quality Management movement.
   c. Data that deal more with opinions than statistics.

4. It is important to obtain information for evaluation because
   a. Otherwise, we may not have a sense of the big picture.
   b. Management prefers interpretation to hard facts.
   c. Turf wars could erupt unless we do.

5. Which of these statements about a focus group is not true?
   a. There should be an agenda.
   b. A neutral party should serve as facilitator.
   c. The ideal size is about 12 people.

6. When you fine-tune a solution, you
   a. Determine the process variables.
   b. Make adjustments.
   c. Scrap the process and start from scratch.

Step 5: Evaluating the Solution

7. Which of the following is a question that should be asked to determine lessons learned?
   a. What was an unexpected benefit?
   b. Was consensus satisfactorily obtained?
   c. Were convergence techniques used in "imagineering" (using the imagination to engineer improvements)?

8. P-D-C-A stands for
   a. Preview-Develop-Confirm-Achieve.
   b. Plan-Do-Check-Act.
   c. Prepare-Delegate-Confirm-Assess.

• **Step 6: Improving Continuously**

Chapter *Eight*

Step 6: Improving Continuously

> **Chapter Objectives**
> ▶ Engage in a benchmarking project.
> ▶ Set "stretch" goals.

In Chapter 2, we examined the cyclical nature of the problem-solving process. You may remember that Step 6, Improve Continuously, brings the process back full circle to defining new problems and generating their solutions.

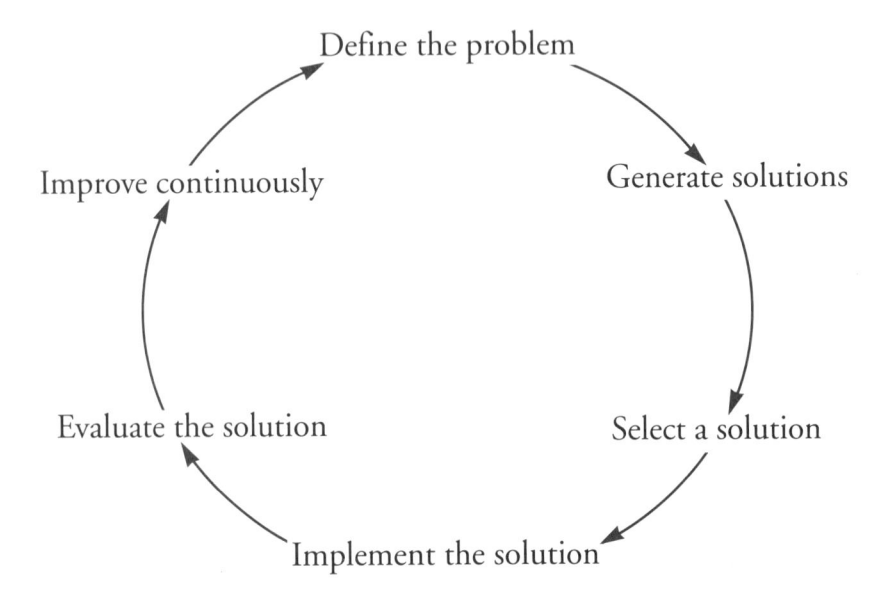

```
              Define the problem
         ↗                        ↘
Improve continuously          Generate solutions
         ↑                        ↓
Evaluate the solution          Select a solution
         ↖                        ↙
            Implement the solution
```

Why is Continuous Improvement so important to the problem-solving process? Successful people and organizations know they must always be on the lookout for new ways to make themselves better, increase their competitive advantage, eliminate waste, and widen revenue streams. Such thinking is at the heart of Continuous Improvement.

Step 6: Improving Continuously

Continuous Improvement Through Benchmarking

Many methods lead to improvement. One method, *benchmarking,* means posing the question "How can we be better than we are?" and answering "By learning how the best in our field do what they do." No matter what the problem, others have faced similar situations and found successful solutions. When we study their solutions and apply them to our own situations, we are engaging in benchmarking. To be sure, we can solve problems on our own, without input from those who may be one step ahead of us. Certainly, we can deny outside help and invent or reinvent solution wheels all by ourselves. But it makes more sense to study and learn from examples of excellence than to invest time, money, and effort unnecessarily.

The Xerox Corporation learned to expedite ordering by studying not another copier company but the L. L. Bean catalog company, known far and wide for accuracy and rapidity in fulfilling customer orders. Taiichi Ohno, the Japanese manufacturer who introduced the "just-in-time" concept, came upon that idea after visiting an American supermarket.

Excellence abounds. By making a studied effort to understand how others acquired it and by benchmarking with outstanding exemplars, we facilitate our own acquisition of excellence.

Engaging in a Benchmarking Project

Benchmarking is a process of comparing ourselves to others in order to improve what we are doing. As we review our actions and compare our outcomes to higher achievers, we may discover that even solutions that turned out well might be made better the next time around. "If it ain't broke, don't fix it" used to be an American management mantra. More and more, however, converts are chanting a different refrain today: "If it ain't broke, break it!" Such sentiments are reflected in advertisements for Lexus cars, a company that prides itself on "the relentless pursuit of perfection."

Benchmarking is an effective way to gauge the excellence of our endeavors and inspire ourselves to even higher levels of perfection in the solutions we implement and the decisions we

Step 6: Improving Continuously

make. Very likely, others face the same problems we do. Before implementing solutions that require significant amounts of time, money, and effort to measure and monitor, we can contact others in similar circumstances to learn how they solved similar problems. By learning about their best practices, we discover what makes organizations famous as they produce their products or add value to the service they offer customers.

Twelve different companies might offer the same product or service, yet one firm is probably outstanding in the way it reduced cycle time, or expanded markets, or increased profits, or made creative use of technology. On an individual level, imagine 12 people who do essentially the same work. To be sure, they do not all work in the same way. One or more has inevitably developed a best practice: he or she has discovered a shortcut, a way to save money, a way to avoid duplicated effort, or a way to make customers more satisfied. By studying both corporate and individual examples of best practices, continuous improvement becomes a way of life.

Benchmarking consists of the following four steps:

1. **Conduct an assessment.**
   Analyze the way things are currently done in your organization and record how processes operate. Determine what things are well done and what things are not well done. Decide what customers really want and what is being done to give them what they want. Know what questions to ask your benchmarking partner.

2. **Find a partner.**
   The person or organization from which you wish to obtain comparative knowledge need not be in the same type of business you are. Learn what you can about exemplary organizations in your area and in other areas where you can afford to travel. Obtain permission from your own management before contacting other companies and have your plan ready for management approval. Consider the cost of on-site visits and decide what information can be acquired by other means. Once decisions are made, partners can be contacted and partnerships can be formed. Gather data for subsequent analysis.

Step 6: Improving Continuously

3. **Transfer learning.**
    With benchmarking data in hand, individuals or teams decide how the new knowledge can be most profitably transferred to their own circumstances. In particular, they review what was being done better by the benchmark partner and explore the transferability of those practices. Benchmarking visits allow the discovery of practices in our own organization that need no longer be continued and others not being done that perhaps should be.

4. **Evaluate the transfers.**
    After extensively monitoring new practices, benchmarkers or benchmarking teams decide what works and what it cost to make it work. They also consider results of newly introduced practices to determine if they should continue. And, in the spirit of continuous improvement, benchmarkers ask "What's next?" Benchmarking opens new vistas of possibility. Individuals, teams, and organizations must give careful and deliberate thought to steps that follow the acquisition of knowledge. Will we apply the learning to our own circumstances? How fully do we intend to implement the excellence we observed? To what extent do we wish to commit ourselves to improvement? Do we have sufficient resources to replicate outstanding practices we discovered? Do we need to set stretch goals?

Setting "Stretch" Goals

"Stretch" goals challenge us to raise the bar of excellence. If we are serious about bringing positive change into our lives and into our organizations, then we are serious about setting goals that encourage growth. We solve problems not merely to find solutions, but to ensure those solutions yield results aligned with individual aims and organizational missions. To obtain the best results, we may need to change our minds as well as our mind-sets; we may need to abandon the old and embrace the new; we may even need to broaden goals that no longer constitute excellence. These shifts in attitude are often prompted by benchmarking experiences.

From the world of Total Quality Management comes a popular maxim: "If you always do what you've always done, you'll always be what you already are." However, when you stretch, you go beyond what you already are to what you can become.

Step 6: Improving Continuously

In helping yourself, your team, or your organization to stretch, you will need to:

- **Build a support network.** Include individuals/organizations like yourself and unlike yourself. Select those who have demonstrated excellence in a given field.

- **Plan a strategy.** The popular saying, "If you don't know where you're going, any road will take you there," certainly applies here. With a destination in mind, you need a road map to help you reach it.

- **Set deadlines.** Goals must be measurable, if only in terms of time. Without deadlines, we tend to drift along until one day we discover it is far too late to achieve the promises we made to ourselves and/or to others.

- **Celebrate your successes.** Reward yourself for the hard work that led to mini-goal accomplishments along the way to the maxi-goal. Celebrations are as important to individuals as they are to teams and entire organizations.

- **Record results.** While progressing through the Wheel of Improvement individually and together, collect data to determine the success of your efforts. After going "full-circle" and before starting the cycle anew, take a moment to reflect on what worked and what didn't work.

- **Do your homework.** Gathering data, learning about new approaches, asking questions, studying other operations—all these knowledge-acquisition processes constitute the homework required to make us ready for new input.

- **Overcome fear.** Yes, fear always appears at the beginning of a new undertaking. Fear also accompanies every stage along the way. And, at the end, fear of failure or even fear of success may raise its ugly head. Self-talk and team-talk can eradicate some fear. Talking to others who faced and conquered similar doubts also helps overcome the plague of negative emotions.

- **Evaluate risks.** Each point on the improvement wheel is associated with risk. Take time to evaluate and discuss the risks with knowledgeable associates. If you decide the risks are excessive, find alternatives that yield results without jeopardizing gains.

Step 6: Improving Continuously

Take a Moment

Imagine your improvement goal in the center of a circle—a Wheel of Improvement. To reach that centered and central goal, you must take many steps. Their order depends upon the opportunities that present themselves and the priorities relevant to differing circumstances.

On the following diagram, look at the goal spokes that form the Wheel of Improvement. In the center, write your improvement goal or the problem you hope to solve. On each spoke line, write one specific thing you can do in each step outside the wheel. Begin with "Build a support network." In the circle above that step, tell how, or with whom, or by when you could establish such support. Continue clockwise around the wheel, recording at least one concrete "how" for each "what."

By working through the entire circle and following each step, your goal should be within reach. If not, review the weakest spoke and strengthen it in the next cycle. As you do, know that good enough seldom is. Because today's effective solutions may not work with tomorrow's problems, improvement steps are shown in the form of a wheel, a wheel that keeps on turning, forcing us repeatedly through the same process in order to achieve ever-improving outcomes.

Wheel of Improvement

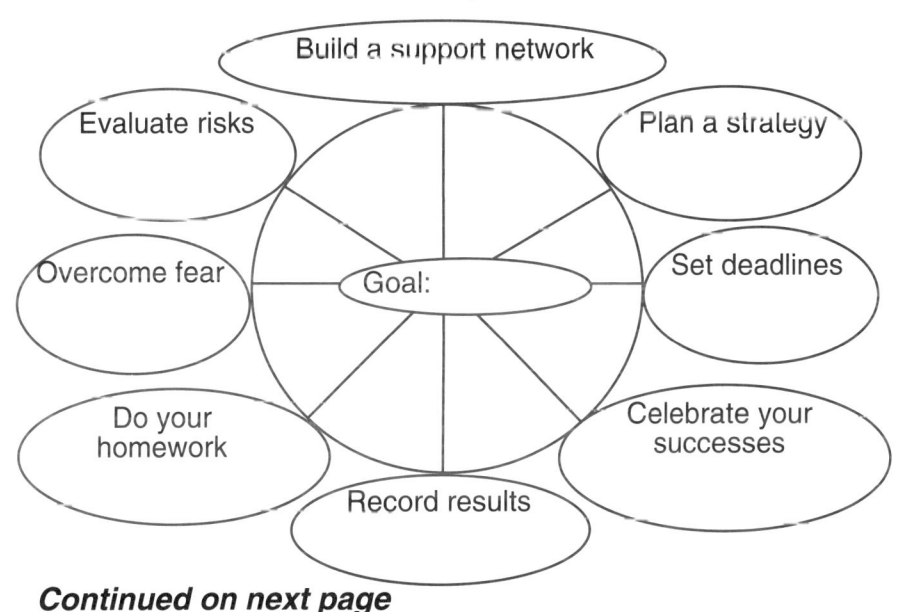

- Build a support network
- Plan a strategy
- Set deadlines
- Celebrate your successes
- Record results
- Do your homework
- Overcome fear
- Evaluate risks

Goal:

Continued on next page

Step 6: Improving Continuously

> **Take a Moment** *(continued)*
>
> To spur yourself and/or your team to ever-greater problem-solving achievement, draw improvement wheels each time new difficulties arise. Make the circle bigger and the goal more ambitious each time. Post improvement wheels in your office or in the room used by the team for problem-solving meetings to provide visual inspiration, not only for ongoing problem-solving efforts, but also to provide underlying motivation and stretch the possibilities associated with solutions you implement.

Chapter Summary

Growth potential is the primary ingredient in the recipe for our last step, Step 6, Improving Continuously. If we seriously want to develop our own skills, our team's output, our department's processes, and our organization's service to customers, then we will embark upon a benchmarking journey. Four steps are involved.

1. Conduct an assessment of our existing processes.

2. Find a benchmarking partner and visit the partner's site.

3. Transfer what we learned to our own operation.

4. Evaluate the effectiveness of the transferred practices.

Benchmarking pushes us to set stretch goals for ourselves. Setting stretch goals often pushes us to benchmark further. The benchmarking process, like the problem-solving process, is designed with a singular aim in mind: the improvement of existing practices.

Step 6: Improving Continuously

Self-Check: Chapter 8 Review

Complete the following dialogue between two coworkers. Tom is eager to learn more about Continuous Improvement. Raquel is telling him what she knows about benchmarking and setting stretch goals. When your dialogue is complete (with at least 10 lines of script for each character), compare what you wrote about benchmarking and setting stretch goals to what appeared in Chapter 8.

Tom:
My boss suggested in my performance appraisal that I give some serious thought to "Continuous Improvement," and I'm not even sure what that means.

Raquel:
If you have a few minutes, I'd be happy to tell you what I've learned recently.

Tom:
Are you serious? That would be great!

Raquel:
Let's start with the concept of "Benchmarking."

_____

_____

Tom:

_____

_____

Raquel:

_____

_____

119

Answers to Selected Exercises

Chapter 1

Take a Moment (page 16)

1. C
2. C
3. C
4. D
5. L

Chapter Review (page 20)

1. *Convergent* thinking can be equated with scientific thinking or precise logical thought. *Divergent* thinking is more spontaneous or creative. *Lateralized* refers to the ability to use both types of thinking equally well.

2. a. Define the problem.
   b. Generate possible solutions.
   c. Select a solution.
   d. Implement the solution.
   e. Evaluate the solution.

3. It is better to be lateralized because different problems require different kinds of thinking for their solutions.

4. Two ways to develop convergent skills are gauging the time it will take to do things and learning more about finance.

5. To enhance divergent thinking skills, one could engage in "What if . . ." thinking and take an art class.

Chapter 2

Chapter Review (page 36)

1. Occasionally substitute the words *challenge* or *opportunity* for the word *problem*.

2. Determine the overall importance of the problem and allocate your time accordingly.

Answers to Selected Exercises

3. a. What are the possible causes of this situation?
   b. Which of these problems are causes in themselves?
   c. What concerns surround these problems?
   d. What aspects of the situation are not actual problems?

4. The Five-Why Technique involves probing the problem by continuing to ask the question "Why?" until the root cause is finally uncovered.

5. We will generate the most effective solution to a problem if we consider the perspectives of all those affected by the problem, as well as the perspectives of unaffected people who can give us new insights.

Chapter 3

Chapter Review (page 51)

All answers were False. Here are the reasons why.
1. Research shows we are all capable of remarkable creativity.
2. *Janusian* refers to considering a situation or problem from two opposing points of view.
3. About one-third of our reading should be spent reading about things outside our field of interest.

4. The steps are:
   a. Describe the problem.
   b. Compare it to something.
   c. List the features of the thing to which you compared the problem.
   d. Review the list of features and choose one that sums up the problem for you. Ask yourself what solutions this feature suggests.

5. a. Spontaneous Thoughts
   b. Work Thoughts
   c. People Thoughts
   d. Workable Solutions

Answers to Selected Exercises

Chapter Four

Chapter Review (page 67)

1. b
2. f
3. a
4. e
5. c
6. d

Chapter 5

Thinking "Outside the Box" (page 82)

In this diagram, the letter "t" is clearly out of place. Not only is it bigger than any of the other letters, but it is also represented by a dotted line, while the others are uniform in their font and size.

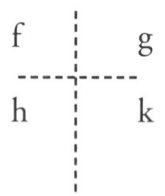

```
    f   ┊   g
  ------+------
    h   ┊   k
        ┊
```

Chapter Review (page 88)

1. P=Popularity Evaluation
   O=Optimization Level Assessment
   W=Worth Assessment

2. a. State the problem and brainstorm possible solutions.
   b. Reduce an original list of 20+ choices to 10 top choices.
   c. Compare each choice to all the other choices.
   d. Determine the Optimization Level for each possible solution.
   e. Determine the Worth Level for each option.
   f. Average the team's Optimization percentages.
   g. Average the team's Worth ratings.
   h. Plot the values on a grid.
   i. Analyze the results.

Answers to Selected Exercises

Chapter 6

Chapter Review (page 99)

1. a. Melt
   b. Change
   c. Solidify

2. The 5-X Strategy involves:

   EXpect—Anticipate resistance and be prepared to deal with it.

   EXamine the many aspects of the environment affected by the proposed solution. People, whole departments, equipment, schedules, budgets, and so forth need to be considered in terms of the solution's impact.

   EXplain—As comprehensively as possible, make others aware of benefits from the proposed solution. (The WIFM Factor is a powerful force.)

   EXecute—Once all systems are in place, the plan must be executed—carried out according to a carefully prepared strategy.

   EXtend the plan. Find ways to branch out, to benchmark, to garner support from various sources.

Chapter 7

Chapter Review (page 110)

1. b
2. a
3. c
4. a
5. c
6. b
7. a
8. b